MONDAY

IS

MEAT LOAF

and Burgers and Pork Chops and Steaks and More

• • •

TIME-LIFE BOOKS, ALEXANDRIA, VIRGINIA

TIME-LIFE BOOKS IS A DIVISION OF TIME LIFE INC.

PRESIDENT and CEO, Time Life Inc. John M. Fahey Jr.
PRESIDENT, Time-Life Books John D. Hall

TIME-LIFE CUSTOM PUBLISHING
VICE PRESIDENT and PUBLISHER Terry Newell
Director of Sales Neil Levin
Director of New Product Development Regina Hall
Managing Editor Donia Ann Steele
Editorial Director Jennifer Pearce
Senior Art Director Christopher M. Register
Sales Manager Liz Ziehl
Retail Promotions Manager Gary Stoiber
Associate Marketing Manager Dana A. Coleman
Operations Manager Valerie Lewis
Director of Financial Operations J. Brian Birky
Financial Analyst Trish Palini
Production Manager Carolyn Bounds
Quality Assurance Manager Miriam P. Newton
Executive Assistant Tammy York

Produced by Rebus, Inc.
New York, New York

Illustrations
William Neeper

Library of Congress Cataloging-in-Publication Data
Monday is meat loaf and burgers and pork chops and steaks and more.
p. cm. -- (The Everyday cookbooks)
Includes index.
ISBN 0-8094-9186-9
ISBN 0-7835-4776-5
1. Cookery (Meat) 2. Quick and easy cookery. I. Time-Life Books.
II. Series.
TX749.M565   1995
641.6'6--dc20

95-18648
CIP

Introduction

Remember when you could tell what day of the week it was by what Mom was making for dinner? It was predictable, and comforting, and—as far as Mom was concerned—efficient. But every now and then, didn't you wish she would give her usual meat loaf recipe a rest and try something new? Now here's a cookbook that not only helps you plan meals like Mom used to make but gives you a wonderful variety of recipes, too. With *Monday Is Meat Loaf,* you can offer your family a delightfully different main-course meat dish every week.

To make life even easier, this cookbook includes the following features:

- There are no difficult techniques or exotic ingredients. All of the recipes can be made with supermarket-available foods, and a great many of them can be made entirely with ingredients already in the pantry.

- Each recipe is designed with everyone's busy schedule in mind, with most taking under 30 minutes to prepare. These recipes are labeled "Extra-Quick" and are marked with this symbol: ◆ (A full listing of the extra-quick recipes is included in the index under the heading Extra-Quick.)

- Many of the recipes include lower-fat alternatives, such as reduced-fat sour cream and low-fat milk. In addition, we have created a number of recipes that get fewer than 30 percent of their calories from fat. These recipes are labeled "Low-Fat" and are marked with this symbol: ◇ (A full listing of the low-fat recipes is included in the index under the heading Low-Fat.)

- As a further help to the cook, there are notes throughout the book that provide simple variations on recipes, cooking shortcuts or tips on how to lower fat, suggestions for simple desserts that can be made for weekday meals, and substitutions, in case you can't find (or don't like) certain ingredients.

- In a special section called "Family Favorites," we include recipes that even the pickiest eaters will like, such as Maple-Glazed Pork Chops with Roasted Potatoes and Roast Eye Round with Mushroom Sauce.

But best of all, in *Monday Is Meat Loaf* there are enough delicious meat recipes for more than two years' worth of Mondays!

Contents

Soups, Stews, and Braises

Hearty Tomato-Meatball Soup   6
Minestrone with Chick-Peas   7
Veal Stew with Onions and Mustard   8
Beef with Peppers and Pasta   9
Quick Chunky Chili   10
Tex-Mex Beef Skillet   11
Beef-Tomato Curry   12
Beef Paprikash over Egg Noodles   13
Light Beef Stew with Asparagus   14
Beef Stew with Couscous   15
Pork Stroganoff   16
Italian Sausage and Squash Stew   17
Lentil-Sausage Stew   18
Swedish Meatballs   19
Beef and Sausage Balls in Spicy Tomato Sauce   20
Apple-Braised Pork Chops with Red Cabbage   21
Pork Chops Braised with Onions   22
Pork in Wine Sauce   23
Kielbasa with Apples, Cabbage, and Celery   24

Sautés and Stir-Fries

Sweet-and-Sour Veal Scaloppini   25
Veal Cutlets with Lemon and Parsley   26
Italian Veal and Peppers   27
Veal Chops with Spinach, Tomatoes, and Peas   28
Veal Chops with Sour Cream-Dill Sauce   29
Beef Bourguignon Sauté   30
Skillet-Roasted Steak with Piquant Sauce   31
Pork Parmesan   32
Pork Cutlets with Zesty Sauce   33
Gingered Pork Cutlets   34
Peppered Pork Steaks with Pears   35
Red Pepper Pork with Mint   36
Pork Chops with Caramelized Apples   37

Pork Chops with Lemon-Soy Sauce Glaze   38
German-Style Pork Chops with Mushrooms   39
Pork Chops with Apples and Onions   40
Pork Chops Diablo   41
Pork Chops with Orange Sauce   42
Pork with Apple-Caraway Cream   43
Sautéed Sausage, Mushrooms, and Peppers   44
Ham Steak with Maple-Bourbon Glaze   45
Beef Tossed with Red Cabbage and Apples   46
Beef and Mushroom Stir-Fry   47
Ginger Orange Beef   48
Stir-Fried Flank Steak and Vegetables   49
Top Round Sautéed with Broccoli and Cauliflower   50
Hawaiian Pork Skillet   51
Orange Pork Stir-Fry   52
Stir-Fried Lamb with Green Beans   53
Spicy Lamb Sauté   54

Baked and Roasted

Oven-Roasted Steak Kebabs with Potatoes   55
Pecan-Mustard Pork Chops   56
Roasted Pork Loin Provençale   57
Bulgur-Stuffed Red Peppers   58
Ham and Swiss Cheese Casseroles   59
Pork-and-Sausage-Stuffed Golden Apples   60
Ham-and-Rice-Stuffed Peppers   61
Beef-and-Onion Shepherd's Pie   62
Cheese Meat Loaf with Parslied Tomato Sauce   63
Italian Meat Loaf with Tomato Sauce   64
Cajun Meat Loaf   65

Grilled and Broiled

Broiled Veal Chops with Winter Vegetable Sauté   66
London Broil with Chili Seasonings   67

London Broil Teriyaki 68

Sirloin Steak with Dijon and Herbed Potatoes 69

London Broil with Caramelized Onions 70

Steak with Lemon-Pepper Crust 71

Herb-Marinated Steak 72

Steak with Horseradish-Mushroom Cream 73

Grilled Steaks with Red Wine-Mushroom Sauce 74

Skirt Steak with Black Bean Chili Sauce 75

Grilled Steaks with Mustard-Yogurt Sauce 76

Sirloin and Leek Skewers with Ginger Chutney 77

Barbecued Beef Kebabs 78

Tomato-Grilled Pork Chops 79

Honey-Apricot Spareribs 80

Indonesian-Style Grilled Pork 81

Broiled Pork Chops with Nectarine Chutney 82

Honey-Glazed Pork Tenderloin 83

Pork Strips with Dipping Sauce 84

Sausage and Potato Kebabs with Mustard Glaze 85

Lamb Chops with Cucumber-Mint Salsa 86

Lamb Shish Kebab with Yogurt Dipping Sauce 87

Burgers and Sandwiches

Milanese Meatball Heros 88

Veal Patties in Parsley Cream Sauce 89

Grilled Beef and Avocados in Flour Tortillas 90

Grilled Beef Gyros with Middle Eastern Salad 91

Light Fajita Roll-Ups 92

Beef Tacos with Fresh Salsa 93

Sloppy Josés 94

Spicy Oriental Hamburgers with Orange Sauce 95

Dijon Burgers with Grilled Onions 96

Herbed Steakburgers 97

Mexican Burgers with Taco Toppings 98

Mini-Beef Patties with Red Pepper Rice 99

Stovetop Barbecued Burgers 100

Lamb Burgers with Basil and Parmesan Sauce 101

Herbed Pork Burgers with Apple-Carrot Relish 102

Chili-Topped Pork Burgers 103

Salads

Mexican Steak Salad 104

Marinated Beef Salad 105

Beef and Tomato Salad 106

Thai Grilled Beef Salad 107

Beef and Barley Salad with Cherry Tomatoes 108

Pork and Ginger Stir-Fry Salad 109

Warm Lentil and Sausage Salad 110

Family Favorites

Beef and Mushroom Soup 111

Easy Veal Stew 112

Chili with No Beans 113

Chuckwagon Beef Stew with Dumplings 114

Three-Pepper Smothered Minute Steak 115

Sausages Pizzaiola 116

Simple Beef Burgundy 117

Pork Chops with Fresh Cranberry Sauce 118

Roast Eye Round with Mushroom Sauce 119

Maple-Glazed Pork Chops with Roasted Potatoes 120

Sweet and Savory Spareribs 121

Broiled Ham with Pineapple and Mustard Glaze 122

Salisbury Steaks with Savory Sauce 123

Cheese-Filled Pepper Burgers 124

Classic Beef Fajitas 125

Index

126

HEARTY TOMATO-MEATBALL SOUP

SERVES 4

2 TABLESPOONS OLIVE OIL

1 SMALL ONION, COARSELY CHOPPED

3 GARLIC CLOVES, MINCED

1 POUND MUSHROOMS, THICKLY
  SLICED

½ TEASPOON SALT

¼ TEASPOON BLACK PEPPER

¾ CUP FRESH BREAD CRUMBS

¼ POUND GROUND PORK TENDERLOIN

¼ POUND GROUND VEAL SHOULDER

1 EGG, LIGHTLY BEATEN

2 CUPS CANNED NO-SALT-ADDED
  WHOLE TOMATOES

2½ CUPS REDUCED-SODIUM CHICKEN
  BROTH

3 TABLESPOONS MINCED FRESH BASIL,
  OR 1 TABLESPOON DRIED

2 TABLESPOONS MINCED FRESH
  OREGANO, OR 2 TEASPOONS DRIED

1 TABLESPOON MINCED FRESH THYME,
  OR 1 TEASPOON DRIED

1. In a large saucepan, warm the oil over low heat. Add the onion and garlic, and cook, stirring frequently, until the onion begins to soften, about 3 minutes.

2. Add the mushrooms, ¼ teaspoon of the salt, and ⅛ teaspoon of the pepper. Increase the heat to high and cook, stirring occasionally, until the mushroom juices have evaporated, about 8 minutes.

3. Meanwhile, in a medium bowl, combine the bread crumbs, pork, veal, beaten egg, and the remaining ¼ teaspoon salt and ⅛ teaspoon pepper, and mix until well blended. Form the mixture into about 20 walnut-size meatballs.

4. Add the tomatoes to the saucepan, breaking them up with the back of a spoon. Increase the heat to high and cook, stirring occasionally, for 5 minutes.

5. Add the broth, basil, oregano, and thyme, and bring the liquid to a boil. Stir in the meatballs, reduce the heat to low, partially cover, and simmer until the meatballs are cooked through, about 30 minutes. Serve hot.

Minestrone with Chick-Peas

SERVES 4 TO 6

¾ OUNCE DRIED MUSHROOMS

2 TABLESPOONS OLIVE OIL

½ POUND BACON, COARSELY CHOPPED

1 BONELESS PORK LOIN CHOP (ABOUT
    ¼ POUND), CHOPPED

3 MEDIUM ONIONS, THINLY SLICED

1 MEDIUM CARROT, FINELY CHOPPED

1 CELERY RIB, FINELY CHOPPED

¼ CUP CHOPPED PARSLEY

2 LARGE GARLIC CLOVES, MINCED

2 TEASPOONS BASIL

¾ TEASPOON OREGANO

1¼ CUPS CANNED TOMATO PURÉE

ONE 16-OUNCE CAN NO-SALT-ADDED
    WHOLE TOMATOES

ONE 15-OUNCE CAN CHICK-PEAS,
    RINSED AND DRAINED

1 MEDIUM ZUCCHINI, DICED

1 CUP BOTTLED ROASTED RED PEPPERS,
    CUT INTO THIN STRIPS

6 CUPS REDUCED-SODIUM CHICKEN
    BROTH

6 OUNCES BROAD NOODLES

½ TEASPOON SALT

¼ TEASPOON BLACK PEPPER

1½ CUPS GRATED PARMESAN CHEESE

1. In a small bowl, cover the dried mushrooms with boiling water, and let soak until softened, about 10 minutes.

2. Meanwhile, in a Dutch oven, warm the oil over medium-high heat. Add the bacon and pork, and cook, stirring frequently, until lightly browned, 5 to 7 minutes.

3. Spoon off all but a thin layer of fat in the pan. Add the onions, carrot, celery, and parsley. Cover, reduce the heat to medium-low, and cook for 10 minutes.

4. With a slotted spoon, transfer the mushrooms to the pan. Strain the mushroom soaking liquid through a fine-mesh sieve into the

pan. Stir in the garlic, basil, and oregano, and simmer for 3 minutes. Add the tomato purée and whole tomatoes. Bring to a boil over medium heat and cook for 5 minutes, breaking up the tomatoes with a spoon.

5. Add the chick-peas, zucchini, and pepper strips, and cook, stirring, for 1 minute. Stir in the broth and return to a boil. Add the noodles and cook, stirring often, until they are just tender, 6 to 8 minutes. Add the salt and pepper, and remove the pan from the heat.

6. Serve the minestrone sprinkled with some of the Parmesan and offer the remaining cheese on the side.

VEAL STEW WITH ONIONS AND MUSTARD

SERVES 4 TO 6

1½ POUNDS VEAL STEW MEAT, CUT
    INTO 1-INCH CUBES
2 CUPS CHICKEN BROTH, PREFERABLY
    REDUCED-SODIUM
½ CUP DRY WHITE WINE
2 SMALL WHOLE, PEELED ONIONS,
    EACH STUCK WITH 2 CLOVES
1 TEASPOON FRESH THYME, OR
    ¼ TEASPOON DRIED

1½ TABLESPOONS UNSALTED BUTTER
¼ CUP FLOUR
1 LARGE CARROT, THINLY SLICED ON
    THE DIAGONAL
½ POUND FROZEN PEARL ONIONS,
    THAWED
1 TABLESPOON GRAINY MUSTARD
¼ CUP HALF-AND-HALF
⅛ TEASPOON WHITE PEPPER

1. In a large pot, combine the veal, broth, 2 cups of water, the wine, and clove-studded onions. Bring to a boil over medium-high heat and skim off any foam that rises to the surface. Add the thyme, reduce the heat to low, partially cover, and simmer until the veal is just tender, about 40 minutes. Remove and discard the onions.

2. In a small saucepan, warm the butter over medium heat until melted. Whisk in the flour and cook the mixture, whisking constantly, for 3 minutes. Gradually add 2 cups of the veal-cooking liquid, whisking constantly, until a smooth mixture results. Pour this liquid into the pot.

3. Increase the heat under the pot to medium-high and bring the mixture to a boil. Reduce the heat to medium-low, add the carrot and pearl onions, and stir in the mustard. Simmer the stew until the vegetables are tender, about 10 minutes.

4. Stir in the half-and-half and pepper, and serve the stew hot.

BEEF WITH PEPPERS AND PASTA

SERVES 4

◆ EXTRA-QUICK ◇ LOW-FAT

2 MEDIUM RED BELL PEPPERS, CUT
   INTO 3 OR 4 FLAT PANELS, CORES
   AND SEEDS DISCARDED
1 TABLESPOON OLIVE OIL
1¼ POUNDS LEAN GROUND ROUND
6 GARLIC CLOVES, THINLY SLICED
2 LARGE ONIONS, FINELY CHOPPED
1 TEASPOON FENNEL SEEDS
½ TEASPOON BLACK PEPPER
¼ TEASPOON SALT
ONE 16-OUNCE CAN NO-SALT-ADDED
   WHOLE TOMATOES

⅓ CUP RED WINE VINEGAR
1 TEASPOON SUGAR
2 SMALL ZUCCHINI, HALVED
   LENGTHWISE AND THINLY SLICED ON
   THE DIAGONAL
¾ POUND PENNE OR OTHER MEDIUM,
   TUBULAR PASTA
1 CUP CHICKEN BROTH, PREFERABLY
   REDUCED-SODIUM
½ CUP (PACKED) FRESH BASIL LEAVES,
   SHREDDED
¼ CUP GRATED PARMESAN CHEESE

1. Preheat the broiler. Place the pepper pieces, skin-side up, on a baking sheet and broil as close to the heat as possible for 10 minutes, or until evenly charred. Transfer the pepper pieces to a bowl and cover with a plate to steam the peppers. Set aside.

2. Meanwhile, in a large skillet, warm the oil over medium-high heat. Add the ground beef, garlic, onions, fennel seeds, ¼ teaspoon of the black pepper, and the salt. Cook, stirring frequently, until the beef begins to brown, about 2 minutes. Add the tomatoes, vinegar, and sugar; break up the tomatoes with the back of a spoon. Reduce the heat to medium-low and simmer, stirring occasionally, for 10 minutes.

3. Peel the peppers and slice them into thin strips, add to the skillet along with the zucchini, and simmer for 5 minutes.

4. Meanwhile, in a large pot of boiling water, cook the pasta until almost al dente according to package directions. Drain and return it to the pot. Pour in the broth, cover the pot, and slowly bring the broth to a simmer, and cook the pasta for 1 minute. Stir in the beef mixture, basil, and remaining ¼ teaspoon black pepper, and simmer, stirring frequently, until most of the liquid is absorbed, 2 to 3 minutes.

5. Transfer the mixture to a large bowl. Sprinkle the Parmesan on top and serve hot.

Quick Chunky Chili

SERVES 4

◆ EXTRA-QUICK

1 POUND LEAN GROUND BEEF

1 MEDIUM ONION, COARSELY CHOPPED

3 GARLIC CLOVES, MINCED

2 TABLESPOONS CHILI POWDER

1½ TEASPOONS OREGANO

¼ TEASPOON BLACK PEPPER

ONE 16-OUNCE CAN NO-SALT-ADDED
   WHOLE TOMATOES

TWO 8-OUNCE CANS TOMATO SAUCE

ONE 15-OUNCE CAN BLACK BEANS,
   RINSED AND DRAINED

1 LARGE GREEN BELL PEPPER, CUT INTO
   ½-INCH PIECES

CHOPPED SCALLIONS, SOUR CREAM,
   AND SHREDDED CHEDDAR, FOR
   GARNISH (OPTIONAL)

1. In a large nonstick skillet over medium-high heat, brown the beef, stirring frequently, until it is no longer pink, about 8 minutes.

2. Add the onion and garlic, and cook, stirring frequently, until the onion is translucent, about 3 minutes. Stir in the chili powder, oregano, and black pepper, and cook, stirring, for 2 minutes. Stir in the tomatoes, tomato sauce, and black beans, and bring the mixture to a boil, breaking up the tomatoes with the back of a spoon.

3. Stir in the bell pepper, reduce the heat to medium-low, cover, and simmer, stirring occasionally, until the flavors have blended, about 15 minutes.

4. Serve the chili hot with bowls of chopped scallions, sour cream, and shredded Cheddar on the side, if desired.

Substitution: *You can usually substitute one kind of canned beans for another. Since the beans are ready to eat as they come from the can, cooking time is not a factor (as it would be with dried beans). You might make this chili with kidney, pinto, or pink beans.*

TEX-MEX BEEF SKILLET

SERVES 4

◆ EXTRA-QUICK

2 TABLESPOONS VEGETABLE OIL
1 MEDIUM ONION, COARSELY CHOPPED
2 GARLIC CLOVES, MINCED
3 TABLESPOONS FLOUR
3 TABLESPOONS CHILI POWDER
¼ TEASPOON BLACK PEPPER
1 POUND FLANK STEAK, CUT WITH THE
  GRAIN INTO 2 STRIPS, THEN ACROSS
  THE GRAIN INTO THIN SLICES

1 LARGE GREEN BELL PEPPER, DICED
1 LARGE YELLOW OR RED BELL PEPPER,
  DICED
ONE 15-OUNCE CAN BLACK BEANS,
  RINSED AND DRAINED
⅔ CUP BEEF BROTH
2 TEASPOONS WORCESTERSHIRE SAUCE
½ TEASPOON OREGANO
¼ TEASPOON SALT

1. In a large skillet, warm 1 tablespoon of the oil over medium-high heat. Add the onion and garlic, and cook, stirring frequently, until the mixture is golden, about 5 minutes. Transfer the garlic-onion mixture to a plate and set aside.

2. In a plastic or paper bag, combine the flour, chili powder, and black pepper, and shake to mix. Add the steak and shake to coat lightly. Remove the steak and reserve 1 tablespoon of the excess seasoned flour.

3. Add the remaining 1 tablespoon oil to the skillet and warm over medium-high heat. Add the steak and cook, stirring frequently, until the beef is browned but still slightly pink in the center, about 4 minutes.

4. Stir in the reserved seasoned flour and cook, stirring constantly, until the flour is no longer visible, about 1 minute.

5. Return the garlic-onion mixture to the skillet. Add the bell peppers, beans, broth, ⅓ cup of water, the Worcestershire sauce, oregano, and salt. Bring the mixture to a boil and cook, stirring constantly, until the bell peppers are tender and the liquid thickens slightly, 2 to 3 minutes.

6. Serve the stew hot.

BEEF-TOMATO CURRY

SERVES 4

1 CUP RICE

¼ CUP BEEF BROTH

3 TABLESPOONS REDUCED-SODIUM SOY
SAUCE

2 TEASPOONS CORNSTARCH

¼ TEASPOON BLACK PEPPER

2 TABLESPOONS VEGETABLE OIL

1 MEDIUM ONION, CUT INTO WEDGES

3 QUARTER-SIZE SLICES FRESH GINGER,
FINELY CHOPPED

3 GARLIC CLOVES, MINCED

1 POUND FLANK STEAK, CUT WITH THE
GRAIN INTO 2 STRIPS, THEN ACROSS
THE GRAIN INTO THIN SLICES

¼ CUP CURRY POWDER

1 POUND FRESH PLUM TOMATOES,
QUARTERED, OR ONE 16-OUNCE
CAN NO-SALT-ADDED WHOLE
TOMATOES, DRAINED AND CHOPPED

1 LARGE GREEN BELL PEPPER, CUT INTO
¾-INCH SQUARES

1. In a medium saucepan, combine the rice and 2 cups of water. Bring to a boil over medium-high heat, reduce the heat to low, cover, and simmer until the rice is tender, about 20 minutes.

2. Meanwhile, in a small bowl, stir together the broth, soy sauce, cornstarch, and black pepper. Set aside.

3. In a large skillet, warm 1 tablespoon of the oil over medium-high heat. Add the onion, ginger, and garlic, and cook, stirring frequently, until the onion begins to brown, about 3 minutes.

4. Add the beef and 2 tablespoons of the curry powder, and stir-fry until the beef is

browned but still slightly pink in the center, about 3 minutes. Transfer the beef mixture to a plate and set aside.

5. Add the remaining 1 tablespoon oil, 2 tablespoons curry powder, and the tomatoes to the skillet. Cook, stirring constantly, for 1 minute. Add the bell pepper and cook, stirring, until it is crisp-tender, about 3 minutes.

6. Return the beef mixture to the skillet. Stir in the reserved broth mixture and bring to a boil. Cook, stirring constantly, until the beef and vegetables are tender and the sauce is slightly thickened, about 2 minutes.

7. Serve the curry over the cooked rice.

Beef Paprikash
over Egg Noodles

SERVES 4

⅓ CUP FLOUR

2 TABLESPOONS PAPRIKA

¼ TEASPOON SALT

¼ TEASPOON BLACK PEPPER

1 POUND STEW BEEF, CUT INTO
   ¾-INCH CHUNKS

2 TABLESPOONS OLIVE OIL

1 MEDIUM ONION, THINLY SLICED

3 GARLIC CLOVES, MINCED

ONE 14½-OUNCE CAN NO-SALT-ADDED
   STEWED TOMATOES

¼ CUP BEEF BROTH

2 TEASPOONS WORCESTERSHIRE SAUCE

1 LARGE RED BELL PEPPER, CUT INTO
   BITE-SIZE PIECES

½ POUND EGG NOODLES

1 TABLESPOON UNSALTED BUTTER

⅓ CUP REDUCED-FAT SOUR CREAM

1. In a plastic or paper bag, combine the flour, paprika, salt, and black pepper, and shake to mix. Add the beef and shake to coat lightly. Remove the beef and reserve the excess seasoned flour.

2. In a large skillet, warm 1 tablespoon of the oil over medium-high heat. Add the onion and garlic, and cook, stirring frequently, until the mixture begins to brown, about 3 minutes. Transfer to a plate and set aside.

3. Add the remaining 1 tablespoon oil to the skillet and warm over medium-high heat. Add the beef and cook, stirring frequently, until browned all over, about 5 minutes. Return the onion mixture to the skillet along with the re-served seasoned flour and cook, stirring constantly, until the flour is no longer visible, about 30 seconds.

4. Add the stewed tomatoes, beef broth, and Worcestershire sauce, and bring the mixture to a boil. Add the bell pepper, reduce the heat to low, cover, and simmer while you cook the noodles.

5. In a large pot of boiling water, cook the noodles until al dente according to package directions.

6. Drain the noodles well and toss them with the butter. Serve the noodles topped with the stew and a dollop of the sour cream.

LIGHT BEEF STEW WITH ASPARAGUS

SERVES 4

◇ LOW-FAT

1 CUP RICE

¼ CUP FLOUR

¼ TEASPOON BLACK PEPPER

¾ POUND TOP ROUND STEAK, CUT
    INTO 1-INCH CHUNKS

1 TABLESPOON OLIVE OIL

1½ CUPS BEEF BROTH

1 POUND SMALL RED POTATOES, CUT
    INTO 1-INCH CHUNKS

3 MEDIUM CARROTS, CUT INTO 1-INCH
    CHUNKS

2 GARLIC CLOVES, MINCED

1½ TEASPOONS THYME

1 BAY LEAF

½ POUND ASPARAGUS, CUT INTO
    1-INCH LENGTHS

8 SCALLIONS, COARSELY CHOPPED

1. In a medium saucepan, combine the rice and 2 cups of water. Bring to a boil over medium-high heat, reduce the heat to low, cover, and simmer until the rice is tender, about 20 minutes.

2. Meanwhile, in a shallow bowl, combine the flour and pepper. Dredge the beef lightly in the seasoned flour, reserving the excess seasoned flour.

3. In a large nonstick skillet, warm the oil over medium-high heat. Add the beef and cook, stirring frequently, until the meat is browned, about 6 minutes.

4. Stir the reserved seasoned flour into the skillet and cook, stirring constantly, until the flour is no longer visible, about 30 seconds. Stir in the broth, potatoes, carrots, garlic, thyme, and bay leaf. Bring to a boil, reduce the heat to low, cover, and simmer until the potatoes are tender, 15 to 20 minutes.

5. Discard the bay leaf. Return the stew to a boil over medium-high heat. Add the asparagus and scallions, and cook until the asparagus is just tender, about 5 minutes.

6. Serve the stew over the cooked rice.

BEEF STEW WITH COUSCOUS

SERVES 4

◇ LOW - FAT

½ TEASPOON SALT

½ TEASPOON BLACK PEPPER

1 POUND STEWING BEEF, CUT INTO
   1-INCH CUBES

2 TABLESPOONS FLOUR

1 TABLESPOON OLIVE OIL

1 SMALL ONION, THINLY SLICED

1 GARLIC CLOVE, MINCED

½ CUP DRY VERMOUTH

½ TEASPOON CINNAMON

1 CUP DRIED APRICOTS, HALVED

3 CUPS REDUCED-SODIUM CHICKEN
   BROTH

1 CUP FROZEN PEAS

1 CUP QUICK-COOKING COUSCOUS

1. Sprinkle ¼ teaspoon of the salt and the pepper over the beef cubes, then dredge them in the flour, shaking off the excess.

2. In a large Dutch oven, warm the oil over medium-high heat. Add the beef and cook, turning frequently, until browned on all sides, about 3 minutes.

3. Push the beef to one side of the pan, reduce the heat to medium, and add the onion and garlic. Cook, stirring frequently, until the onion is translucent, about 4 minutes. Add the vermouth and cinnamon, and stir to scrape up any browned bits clinging to the bottom of the pan. Simmer the liquid until it thickens slightly, 2 to 3 minutes.

4. Stir in ⅓ cup of the apricots and 1½ cups of the broth. Reduce the heat to medium-low,

bring the liquid to a gentle simmer, cover, and cook for 20 minutes. Stir in the remaining 1½ cups broth, cover, and cook until the beef is tender, about 10 minutes.

5. Uncover the stew, stir in the remaining ⅔ cup apricots, and cook for 5 minutes. Stir in the peas and cook until the peas are just heated through, about 3 minutes.

6. Meanwhile, prepare the couscous. In a small saucepan, bring 1½ cups of water and the remaining ¼ teaspoon salt to a boil. Remove the pan from the heat, stir in the couscous, cover, and let stand for 5 minutes.

7. Fluff the couscous with a fork and divide it among 4 shallow bowls. Spoon the beef stew on top and serve hot.

PORK STROGANOFF

SERVES 4

◆ EXTRA-QUICK

1½ TABLESPOONS OLIVE OIL

1 POUND PORK TENDERLOIN, CUT INTO
   THIN STRIPS

1 LARGE ONION, QUARTERED AND
   THINLY SLICED

½ POUND MUSHROOMS, SLICED

2 TABLESPOONS FLOUR

½ C

1¼ CUPS CHICKEN BROTH, PREFERABLY
   REDUCED-SODIUM

1 TABLESPOON TOMATO PASTE

1 TEASPOON FRESH LEMON JUICE

¼ TEASPOON SALT

¼ TEASPOON BLACK PEPPER

¼ CUP PLAIN LOW-FAT YOGURT

1. In a large skillet, warm the oil over medium-high heat. Add the pork strips and onion, and cook, stirring frequently, until the pork is browned all over, about 3 minutes. Stir in the mushrooms and cook, stirring frequently, for 1 minute.

2. Stir in the flour and cook, stirring constantly, until the flour is no longer visible, about 30 seconds. Gradually stir in the broth and bring to a boil, stirring constantly. Reduce the heat to low and simmer for 2 minutes.

3. Stir in the tomato paste, lemon juice, salt, and pepper, and cook until the flavors are blended, about 2 minutes. Remove the pan from the heat, stir in the yogurt until well combined, and serve hot.

KITCHEN NOTE: *Like many great Russian dishes, stroganoff is traditionally enriched with sour cream. Replacing the sour cream with yogurt subtracts about 9 grams of fat from the finished dish.*

Italian Sausage and Squash Stew

SERVES 4

1 POUND SWEET ITALIAN SAUSAGE, CASINGS REMOVED, CUT INTO 1-INCH CHUNKS

1 MEDIUM ONION, COARSELY CHOPPED

3 GARLIC CLOVES, MINCED

½ CUP RICE

ONE 16-OUNCE CAN NO-SALT-ADDED WHOLE TOMATOES

1¾ CUPS CHICKEN BROTH, PREFERABLY REDUCED-SODIUM

2 TABLESPOONS TOMATO PASTE

1 TEASPOON BASIL

1 TEASPOON OREGANO

¼ TEASPOON BLACK PEPPER

1 BAY LEAF

2 TABLESPOONS UNSALTED BUTTER, AT ROOM TEMPERATURE

2 TABLESPOONS FLOUR

1 MEDIUM ZUCCHINI, HALVED LENGTHWISE AND CUT CROSSWISE INTO THIN HALF-ROUNDS

1 MEDIUM YELLOW SQUASH, HALVED LENGTHWISE AND CUT CROSSWISE INTO THIN HALF-ROUNDS

1. In a large saucepan, cook the sausage over medium-high heat, stirring frequently, until evenly browned, 10 to 12 minutes. Drain off all but a thin layer of fat.

2. Add the onion and garlic, and cook, stirring frequently, until the mixture is browned, about 5 minutes.

3. Add the rice, tomatoes, broth, tomato paste, basil, oregano, pepper, and bay leaf, and bring to a boil over medium-high heat, breaking up the tomatoes with the back of a spoon. Reduce the heat to medium-low, cover, and simmer for 15 minutes.

4. Meanwhile, using your fingers, thoroughly blend the butter and flour.

5. Uncover the stew and return it to a boil over medium-high heat. Add the zucchini and yellow squash, and cook until the vegetables are crisp-tender, 5 to 7 minutes.

6. Pinching off about 1 tablespoon at a time, add the butter-flour mixture to the stew, stirring well after each addition. Cook until the stew has thickened slightly, 1 to 2 minutes.

7. Remove the bay leaf and serve the stew hot.

Lentil-Sausage Stew

SERVES 4

3 OUNCES CHORIZO SAUSAGE, CASINGS
   REMOVED AND CUT INTO
   MATCHSTICKS
1 LARGE ONION, MINCED
1½ CUPS LENTILS
3 CUPS REDUCED-SODIUM CHICKEN
   BROTH

2 CELERY RIBS, THINLY SLICED
1 LARGE CARROT, THINLY SLICED
1 TABLESPOON CHOPPED FRESH BASIL,
   OR 2 TEASPOONS DRIED
½ TEASPOON SALT
¼ TEASPOON BLACK PEPPER

1. In a large saucepan, cook the chorizo over medium-low heat for 3 minutes. Add the onion and cook, stirring frequently, until the onion is translucent, about 6 minutes.

2. Stir in the lentils, broth, and 3 cups of water. Bring the liquid to a simmer, cover, and cook until the lentils are tender, about 35 minutes.

3. Stir in the celery, carrot, basil, salt, and pepper. Cover and simmer until the carrot is tender, 7 to 10 minutes. Serve hot.

Kitchen Note: *The spicy sausage called chorizo, seasoned with chilies, oregano, and cumin, is used in both Mexican and Spanish cuisines. Mexicans make chorizo from fresh pork; Spanish chorizo is made from smoked pork. For this recipe, use Spanish-style chorizo, which is firm and sliceable.*

SWEDISH MEATBALLS

SERVES 4

3 TABLESPOONS UNSALTED BUTTER

½ CUP MINCED ONION

1 CUP FRESH BREAD CRUMBS

½ CUP COLD MILK

1 TEASPOON CARAWAY SEEDS

¾ TEASPOON SALT

¾ TEASPOON BLACK PEPPER

½ TEASPOON ALLSPICE

1 EGG

1 POUND LEAN GROUND BEEF, WELL
CHILLED

½ POUND LEAN GROUND PORK, WELL
CHILLED

2 TABLESPOONS FLOUR

1 CUP HALF-AND-HALF

¾ CUP BEEF BROTH

1 TEASPOON WORCESTERSHIRE SAUCE

1. Preheat oven to 400°. Line a roasting pan with foil.

2. In a small skillet, warm 1 tablespoon of the butter over medium heat until melted. Add the onion and cook, stirring frequently, until tender, about 5 minutes.

3. In a large bowl, combine the onion, bread crumbs, milk, caraway seeds, ½ teaspoon each of the salt and pepper, the allspice, and egg; mix well. Add the beef and pork and mix well.

4. Using about a teaspoonful of mixture for each meatball, shape the mixture into about 40 small meatballs and place in the prepared roasting pan. Bake, turning once, for 12 to 15 minutes, or until the meatballs are cooked through and firm when pressed.

5. Meanwhile, in a large skillet, warm the remaining 2 tablespoons butter over medium heat until melted. Add the flour and cook, stirring constantly, for 30 seconds. Add the half-and-half and broth, and bring to a boil, whisking constantly. Cook, whisking, until the gravy is thickened, about 5 minutes. Whisk in the Worcestershire sauce and the remaining ¼ teaspoon each salt and pepper.

6. Add the meatballs and bring the mixture to a boil over medium-high heat. Reduce the heat to medium-low, cover, and simmer until the meatballs are hot, about 10 minutes.

7. Divide the meatballs and gravy among 4 plates and serve hot.

BEEF AND SAUSAGE BALLS in SPICY TOMATO SAUCE

SERVES 4

½ POUND SWEET ITALIAN SAUSAGE, CASINGS REMOVED

½ POUND LEAN GROUND BEEF

¼ CUP FINE UNSEASONED DRY BREAD CRUMBS

¼ CUP GRATED PARMESAN CHEESE

1 TABLESPOON OLIVE OIL

1 MEDIUM ONION, COARSELY CHOPPED

2 GARLIC CLOVES, MINCED

ONE 16-OUNCE CAN CRUSHED TOMATOES

1 TABLESPOON TOMATO PASTE

1 BAY LEAF

½ TEASPOON BASIL

¼ TEASPOON BLACK PEPPER

¼ TEASPOON RED PEPPER FLAKES

1. In a medium bowl, combine the sausage, beef, bread crumbs, and Parmesan, and mix well to blend. Form the mixture into meatballs about 1½ inches in diameter.

2. In a medium saucepan, warm the oil over medium heat. Add the meatballs and brown well on all sides, turning frequently, about 8 minutes.

3. Add the onion and garlic, and cook, stirring frequently, until the onion is translucent, about 2 minutes.

4. Increase the heat to medium-high and stir in the tomatoes, tomato paste, bay leaf, basil, black pepper, and pepper flakes. Cover and bring to a boil. Reduce the heat to medium-low and simmer, stirring occasionally, until the sauce is thickened and the meatballs are cooked through, about 25 minutes.

5. Remove the bay leaf and serve the meatballs and sauce hot.

VARIATION: *Although delicious as is, the meatballs and sauce also make a wonderful pasta topping. Try them, too, spooned into hero rolls to make sandwiches worthy of an Italian street festival.*

APPLE-BRAISED PORK CHOPS WITH RED CABBAGE

SERVES 4

♦ EXTRA-QUICK

1 SMALL UNPEELED GRANNY SMITH
   APPLE, QUARTERED
1 SMALL ONION, QUARTERED
¼ MEDIUM HEAD OF RED CABBAGE,
   HALVED
2 TABLESPOONS CORNSTARCH
½ TEASPOON SALT
½ TEASPOON BLACK PEPPER

4 CENTER-CUT LOIN PORK CHOPS
   (¼ INCH THICK, ABOUT 1 POUND
   TOTAL)
1 TABLESPOON VEGETABLE OIL
½ CUP APPLE JUICE
1 TABLESPOON CIDER VINEGAR
½ TEASPOON CARAWAY SEEDS
½ TEASPOON SUGAR

1. In a food processor with a shredding blade, shred the apple, onion, and cabbage. Set the apple-cabbage mixture aside.

2. In a shallow bowl, combine the cornstarch and ¼ teaspoon each of the salt and pepper. Dredge the pork lightly in the seasoned cornstarch, shaking off the excess. Reserve the excess cornstarch mixture.

3. In a large nonstick skillet, warm the oil over medium-high heat. Add the chops and cook until browned, about 5 minutes per side.

4. Add the apple juice and bring to a boil. Reduce the heat to medium-low, cover, and simmer for 5 minutes. Transfer the chops to a plate; cover loosely with foil to keep warm.

5. Meanwhile, in a small bowl, combine the excess cornstarch mixture and the vinegar.

6. Add the apple-cabbage mixture to the skillet. Increase the heat to medium-high and bring the mixture to a boil.

7. Add the caraway seeds, sugar, and the remaining ¼ teaspoon each salt and pepper. Add the cornstarch mixture and cook, stirring, until the mixture has thickened slightly. Reduce the heat to medium-low, cover, and simmer, stirring occasionally, until the cabbage is just tender, about 5 minutes.

8. Serve the pork chops topped with the cabbage and apple mixture.

PORK CHOPS
BRAISED WITH Onions

SERVES 4

3 TABLESPOONS VEGETABLE OIL

3 MEDIUM ONIONS, THINLY SLICED

4 RIB PORK CHOPS (1 INCH THICK,
  ABOUT 2 POUNDS TOTAL)

¼ TEASPOON SALT

¼ TEASPOON BLACK PEPPER

½ CUP FLOUR

1 TABLESPOON MINCED FRESH THYME
  OR OREGANO, OR 1 TEASPOON
  DRIED

6 TO 8 GARLIC CLOVES, THINLY SLICED

1 CUP CHICKEN BROTH, PREFERABLY
  REDUCED-SODIUM

1. In a large nonstick skillet, warm 1½ tablespoons of the oil over medium heat. Add the onions and cook, stirring frequently, until translucent, about 10 minutes. Transfer to a plate and set aside.

2. Season the pork chops with the salt and pepper. In a shallow dish, combine the flour and thyme. Dredge the chops in the seasoned flour, shaking off the excess.

3. Add the remaining 1½ tablespoons oil to the skillet and warm over medium-high heat. Add the chops and sear for 1 to 2 minutes per side to seal in the juices.

4. Turn the chops and cook until the undersides are golden brown, 3 to 4 minutes. Turn the chops, add the garlic to the pan, and cook until the chops are golden brown on the second side, 3 to 5 minutes, stirring the garlic frequently.

5. Add the broth and reserved onions to the pan. Cover, reduce the heat to low, and cook until the chops are tender and just cooked through, 30 to 40 minutes.

6. Serve the pork chops topped with the onions and pan sauce.

PORK in WINE SAUCE

SERVES 4

1 POUND PORK TENDERLOIN, CUT INTO
1½-INCH-LONG STRIPS

¼ TEASPOON BLACK PEPPER

2 TABLESPOONS OLIVE OIL

2 MEDIUM CARROTS, THINLY SLICED

1 LARGE ONION, CHOPPED

1 MEDIUM LEEK, WHITE PART ONLY,
THINLY SLICED, OR 1 CUP CHOPPED
ONION

1 CUP DRY WHITE WINE

½ CUP CHICKEN BROTH

1 TABLESPOON MINCED FRESH THYME,
OR 1 TEASPOON DRIED

1 TABLESPOON MINCED FRESH
ROSEMARY, OR 1 TEASPOON DRIED

1 BAY LEAF

½ POUND SNOW PEAS

1 TABLESPOON HALF-AND-HALF
(OPTIONAL)

½ POUND TOMATOES, SEEDED AND
SLIVERED

¼ CUP CHOPPED PARSLEY

½ TEASPOON SALT

1. Sprinkle the pork strips with the pepper and rub it in with your fingers. In a flame-proof casserole, warm the oil over high heat. Add the pork, stir vigorously, and cook until browned, about 4 minutes. Transfer to a plate and cover loosely with foil to keep warm.

2. Add the carrots, onion, and leek to the casserole, reduce the heat to low, and cook until the vegetables have softened, about 3 minutes. Add the wine, broth, thyme, rosemary, and bay leaf. Increase the heat to medium-high and bring to a boil. Reduce the heat to low and simmer for 10 minutes, stirring occasionally.

3. Meanwhile, in a medium saucepan of boiling water, blanch the snow peas until they are crisp-tender, about 2 minutes. Drain and rinse under cold running water.

4. Return the pork (and any juices that have collected on the plate) to the casserole and simmer for 5 minutes. Stir in the half-and-half (if using) and cook for 1 minute. Add the snow peas, tomatoes, parsley, and salt, and cook until the tomatoes are just warmed through, about 2 minutes. Serve hot.

Kielbasa with Apples, Cabbage, and Celery

SERVES 4

◆ EXTRA-QUICK

1 POUND KIELBASA OR OTHER FULLY
    COOKED GARLIC SAUSAGE, CUT ON
    THE DIAGONAL INTO ½-INCH SLICES
⅓ CUP APPLE JUICE
⅓ CUP CHICKEN BROTH
1 TABLESPOON CORNSTARCH
½ TEASPOON SAGE
½ TEASPOON CELERY SEED
¼ TEASPOON BLACK PEPPER

1 TABLESPOON PLUS 1 TEASPOON OLIVE
    OIL
1 MEDIUM ONION, COARSELY CHOPPED
3 GARLIC CLOVES, MINCED
3 CUPS SHREDDED CABBAGE
2 MEDIUM UNPEELED GRANNY SMITH
    APPLES, CUT INTO BITE-SIZE PIECES
2 CELERY RIBS, COARSELY CHOPPED

1. In a large saucepan of boiling water, cook the kielbasa for 3 minutes. Drain well and set aside.

2. Meanwhile, in a small bowl, combine the apple juice, broth, cornstarch, sage, celery seed, and pepper. Stir to blend and set aside.

3. In a large skillet, warm 1 tablespoon of the oil over medium-high heat. Add the onion and garlic, and cook, stirring frequently, until the onion begins to brown, about 5 minutes.

4. Add the cabbage, apples, and celery, and cook, stirring, until the vegetables have softened, about 3 minutes. Transfer the sautéed

vegetables to a serving platter and cover loosely with foil to keep warm.

5. In the same skillet, warm the remaining 1 teaspoon oil over medium-high heat. Add the kielbasa and cook, stirring frequently, until it begins to brown, 3 to 4 minutes. Add the cornstarch mixture, bring to a boil, and cook, stirring constantly, until the sauce has thickened slightly, about 2 minutes.

6. Spoon the kielbasa and sauce over the sautéed vegetables. Serve hot.

Sweet-and-Sour Veal Scaloppini

SERVES 4

◆ EXTRA-QUICK

⅓ CUP FLOUR

½ TEASPOON SALT

¼ TEASPOON BLACK PEPPER

8 VEAL CUTLETS (ABOUT 1 POUND
    TOTAL), POUNDED ⅛ INCH THICK

2 TABLESPOONS OLIVE OIL

2 TABLESPOONS UNSALTED BUTTER

½ CUP BEER

½ CUP CHICKEN BROTH

2 TABLESPOONS SPICY BROWN MUSTARD

2 TABLESPOONS BROWN SUGAR

1 TEASPOON DRY MUSTARD

1 TEASPOON THYME

3 TABLESPOONS FRESH LEMON JUICE

1½ TEASPOONS GRATED LEMON ZEST

1. In a shallow bowl, combine the flour, salt, and pepper. Dredge the veal lightly in the seasoned flour, reserving the excess seasoned flour.

2. In a large skillet, warm 1 tablespoon of the oil with 1 tablespoon of the butter over medium-high heat until the butter is melted. Add the veal (in batches if necessary) and cook until browned, about 2 minutes per side, adding the remaining 1 tablespoon oil to prevent sticking. Transfer the veal to a plate and cover loosely with foil to keep warm.

3. Add the remaining 1 tablespoon butter to the pan and warm over medium-high heat until melted. Stir in the reserved seasoned flour and cook, stirring, until the flour is no longer visible, about 30 seconds.

4. Stir in the beer, broth, spicy brown mustard, brown sugar, dry mustard, and thyme. Bring the mixture to a boil, stirring constantly, and cook until slightly thickened, 1 to 2 minutes.

5. Stir in the lemon juice and lemon zest. Return the veal (and any juices that have collected on the plate) to the skillet and bring the mixture to a boil. Reduce the heat to low, cover, and simmer until the veal is cooked through, 1 to 2 minutes.

6. Serve the veal topped with the sauce.

VEAL CUTLETS
WITH LEMON AND PARSLEY

SERVES 4

½ CUP FLOUR

1 POUND VEAL CUTLETS, POUNDED
⅛ INCH THICK

2 TABLESPOONS VEGETABLE OIL

3 TABLESPOONS UNSALTED BUTTER

½ TEASPOON SALT

¼ TEASPOON BLACK PEPPER

3 TABLESPOONS FRESH LEMON JUICE

3 TABLESPOONS CHOPPED PARSLEY

1 LEMON, THINLY SLICED

1. In a shallow bowl, spread the flour. Lightly dredge the cutlets in the flour, shaking off the excess.

2. In a large nonstick skillet, warm the oil and 2 tablespoons of the butter over medium-high heat until the butter is melted. Add as many cutlets as will fit comfortably in a single layer without crowding. Cook until browned, 1 to 2 minutes per side. Sprinkle lightly with some of the salt and pepper, and transfer to a plate. Cover loosely with foil to keep warm. Repeat with the remaining cutlets.

3. Remove the skillet from the heat and add the lemon juice, stirring to scrape up any browned bits clinging to the bottom of the pan. Swirl in the remaining 1 tablespoon butter until melted. Stir in the parsley.

4. Just before serving, return the cooked cutlets to the sauce and heat briefly over low heat, just enough to warm through.

5. Serve the cutlets topped with the pan sauce and garnished with the lemon slices.

Variation: *Other fresh herbs can be used instead of parsley, although the amount substituted will vary. Try tarragon or basil: 1 tablespoon of chopped fresh tarragon or 3 tablespoons of shredded fresh basil. If you use dried herbs, use about one-third the amount of fresh, or 1 teaspoon tarragon and 1 tablespoon basil.*

Italian Veal and Peppers

SERVES 4

½ CUP FLOUR

8 THIN VEAL CUTLETS (ABOUT 1½ POUNDS TOTAL), POUNDED ⅛ INCH THICK

¼ CUP OLIVE OIL

3 TABLESPOONS UNSALTED BUTTER

½ TEASPOON SALT

½ TEASPOON BLACK PEPPER

⅓ CUP DRY WHITE VERMOUTH OR DRY WHITE WINE

3 TABLESPOONS FRESH LEMON JUICE

2 LARGE RED BELL PEPPERS, CUT INTO ½-INCH-WIDE STRIPS

2 LARGE YELLOW BELL PEPPERS, CUT INTO ½-INCH-WIDE STRIPS

1. Spread the flour in a shallow bowl. Lightly dredge half of the cutlets in the flour, shaking off the excess.

2. In a large nonstick skillet, warm 2 tablespoons of the oil and 2 tablespoons of the butter over medium-high heat until the butter is melted. Add the floured cutlets and cook until browned, about 2 minutes per side. Season with ⅛ teaspoon each of the salt and black pepper, transfer to a plate, and cover loosely with foil to keep warm. Dredge the remaining cutlets, sauté, season with ⅛ teaspoon each of the salt and black pepper, and transfer to the plate.

3. Remove the pan from heat and add the vermouth and lemon juice, stirring to scrape up any browned bits clinging to the bottom of the pan.

4. Return the cutlets (and any juices that have collected on the plate) to the pan, cover, and cook over low heat until tender, 20 to 25 minutes.

5. Meanwhile, in a medium skillet, warm the remaining 2 tablespoons oil over high heat. Add the bell peppers and cook, stirring, until well coated with oil, 2 to 3 minutes. Cover the pan, reduce the heat to medium, and cook for 10 minutes. Uncover, add the remaining ¼ teaspoon each salt and pepper, and cook until the bell peppers are very tender, about 8 minutes.

6. Transfer the cutlets to 4 dinner plates and stir the remaining 1 tablespoon butter into the pan. Pour the sauce over the cutlets and serve them topped with the bell peppers.

Veal Chops with Spinach, Tomatoes, and Peas

SERVES 4

¼ CUP FLOUR

¼ TEASPOON BLACK PEPPER

¾ TEASPOON SALT

4 VEAL LOIN CHOPS (½ INCH THICK, ABOUT 1½ POUNDS TOTAL)

2 TABLESPOONS VEGETABLE OIL

1 TEASPOON SAGE

1 MEDIUM ONION, COARSELY CHOPPED

2 GARLIC CLOVES, MINCED

ONE 16-OUNCE CAN NO-SALT-ADDED WHOLE TOMATOES

⅓ CUP CHICKEN BROTH

¼ TEASPOON SUGAR

¼ POUND FRESH SPINACH, CHOPPED, OR HALF A 10-OUNCE PACKAGE FROZEN CHOPPED SPINACH, THAWED AND SQUEEZED DRY

1 CUP FROZEN PEAS

1. In a shallow bowl, combine the flour, pepper, and ½ teaspoon of the salt. Dredge the veal chops lightly in the seasoned flour. Reserve the excess seasoned flour.

2. In a large skillet, warm 1 tablespoon of the oil over medium-high heat. Add the veal and ¾ teaspoon of the sage, and cook until the veal is browned, about 4 minutes per side. Transfer the veal to a plate and cover loosely with foil to keep warm.

3. Add the remaining 1 tablespoon oil to the skillet and warm over medium-high heat. Add the onion and garlic, and cook, stirring frequently, until the onion begins to brown, about 2 minutes.

4. Stir in the reserved seasoned flour and cook, stirring, until the flour is no longer visible, about 30 seconds. Add the tomatoes, breaking them up with the back of a spoon. Add the broth, sugar, and the remaining ¼ teaspoon each salt and sage, and bring to a boil. Reduce the heat, cover, and simmer for 15 minutes.

5. Return the tomato mixture to a boil over medium-high heat. Add the veal chops (and any juices that have collected on the plate), the spinach, and peas, and cook, stirring constantly, until the spinach is wilted and the chops are coated with sauce, about 5 minutes.

6. Serve the chops topped with some of the vegetables and sauce.

28

VEAL CHOPS WITH SOUR CREAM-DILL SAUCE

SERVES 4

2 TABLESPOONS OLIVE OIL

1 LARGE ONION, THINLY SLICED

3 GARLIC CLOVES, MINCED

4 VEAL LOIN CHOPS (½ INCH THICK, ABOUT 1½ POUNDS TOTAL)

1 TABLESPOON PAPRIKA

½ TEASPOON SALT

½ TEASPOON BLACK PEPPER

½ CUP DRY RED WINE OR BEEF BROTH

2 TABLESPOONS RED WINE VINEGAR OR CIDER VINEGAR

1 TABLESPOON UNSALTED BUTTER, AT ROOM TEMPERATURE

1 TABLESPOON FLOUR

⅓ CUP (PACKED) FRESH DILL SPRIGS, MINCED, OR 2 TEASPOONS DRIED

½ TEASPOON SUGAR

⅓ CUP REDUCED-FAT SOUR CREAM

1. In a large skillet, warm 1 tablespoon of the oil over medium-high heat. Add the onion and garlic, and cook, stirring frequently, until the onion begins to brown, about 5 minutes. Transfer the mixture to a plate.

2. Add the remaining 1 tablespoon oil and warm over medium-high heat. Add the veal chops and cook until browned, about 3 minutes per side.

3. Sprinkle in the paprika, salt, and pepper. Add the wine, vinegar, and onion-garlic mixture, and bring to a boil. Reduce the heat to low, cover, and simmer for 10 minutes, stirring the sauce occasionally and turning the chops over halfway through.

4. About 2 minutes before the chops are done, in a small bowl, thoroughly blend the butter and flour.

5. Transfer the chops and onions to a plate and cover loosely with foil to keep warm. Add the dill and sugar to the pan and bring the liquid to a boil over medium-high heat. Pinch off small pieces of the butter-flour mixture and add them to the pan, stirring well after each addition. Cook, stirring, until slightly thickened, about 2 minutes. Remove from the heat and stir in the sour cream.

6. Serve the chops topped with the onions and sour cream-dill sauce.

Beef Bourguignon Sauté

SERVES 4

½ POUND BACON, CUT INTO ½-INCH-
  WIDE STRIPS

1 LARGE ONION, COARSELY CHOPPED

¼ CUP MINCED SHALLOTS OR WHITE
  PART OF SCALLIONS

2 SMALL CARROTS, CUT INTO 2-INCH
  LENGTHS

1½ POUNDS BONELESS TOP SIRLOIN
  STEAK, CUT INTO 1½-INCH CUBES

⅔ CUP DRY RED WINE

1 TEASPOON THYME

¼ TEASPOON SALT

¼ TEASPOON BLACK PEPPER

1 BAY LEAF

12 SMALL MUSHROOMS, QUARTERED OR
  HALVED IF LARGE

1. In a large, wide saucepan, cook the bacon over medium heat until the pan is well coated with fat. Add the onion and shallots, and cook until the bacon is almost crisp and the onion is softened but not browned, about 5 minutes.

2. Add the carrots and beef, increase the heat to medium-high, and cook, stirring, until the beef is browned, about 10 minutes.

3. Stir in the wine, thyme, salt, pepper, and bay leaf. Cover, reduce the heat to low, and simmer until the mixture is fragrant, 10 to 12 minutes, adding some water (or more red wine) if the mixture seems dry.

4. Stir in the mushrooms. Cover and cook until the beef is just cooked and the carrots are crisp-tender, about 5 minutes. (The meat should be rare to medium-rare.)

5. Remove and discard the bay leaf. With a spoon or bulb baster, skim off any visible fat from the surface of the mixture. Transfer the beef and vegetables to a serving platter and serve hot.

Variation: *For a modern twist on this French-style classic, try fresh shiitake mushrooms—which are available in many supermarkets—in place of the button mushrooms called for. Shiitakes have an especially meaty texture and flavor that work well with the robust flavors in this dish.*

Skillet-Roasted Steak with Piquant Sauce

SERVES 4

◆ EXTRA-QUICK

2 TEASPOONS OLIVE OIL

4 SMALL STRIP STEAKS (¾ INCH THICK, ABOUT 1½ POUNDS TOTAL)

½ CUP DRY RED WINE

2 TABLESPOONS TOMATO PASTE

½ TEASPOON HOT PEPPER SAUCE

2 GARLIC CLOVES, MINCED

1 TEASPOON FENNEL SEEDS

½ TEASPOON SUGAR

¼ TEASPOON BLACK PEPPER

½ CUP BEEF BROTH

2 TEASPOONS CORNSTARCH

1. Preheat the oven to 450°.

2. In a large ovenproof skillet, warm the oil over high heat. Add the steaks and sear for 2 minutes per side. Place the skillet in the oven and roast the steaks for 3 minutes. Turn the steaks over and roast for 3 minutes longer, or until medium-rare. Transfer the steaks to a plate and cover loosely with foil to keep warm.

3. Add the wine, tomato paste, hot pepper sauce, garlic, fennel seeds, sugar, and pepper to the skillet, and bring the mixture to a boil over medium-high heat.

4. In a cup, combine the broth and corn-starch, stir into the pan, and cook, stirring constantly, until the sauce thickens slightly, about 2 minutes.

5. Return the steaks (and any juices that have collected on the plate) to the skillet, turning to coat the steaks with the sauce. Serve the steaks topped with the sauce.

PORK PARMESAN

S E R V E S   4

◆ E X T R A - Q U I C K

3 TABLESPOONS FINE UNSEASONED DRY
   BREAD CRUMBS
3 TABLESPOONS GRATED PARMESAN
   CHEESE
1½ TEASPOONS OREGANO
½ TEASPOON BLACK PEPPER

1 EGG WHITE
4 PORK CUTLETS (¼ INCH THICK,
   ABOUT 1¼ POUNDS TOTAL)
2 TABLESPOONS VEGETABLE OIL
1 TABLESPOON UNSALTED BUTTER
1 LEMON, CUT INTO WEDGES

1. In a shallow bowl, combine the bread crumbs, Parmesan, oregano, and pepper. In another shallow bowl, beat the egg white until frothy.

2. Dip the pork cutlets into the egg white, just to coat lightly. Then dip the cutlets into the seasoned bread crumbs, pressing gently to adhere.

3. In a large skillet, warm 1 tablespoon of the oil with the butter over medium-high heat until the butter is melted. Add the pork and cook until golden brown and cooked through, about 3 minutes per side, adding the remaining 1 tablespoon oil, as necessary, to prevent sticking.

4. Serve the cutlets with the lemon wedges on the side.

SUBSTITUTION: *This dish can be made with the turkey cutlets now widely available in supermarkets. Buy thin-sliced cutlets—the cooking time will be the same as for the pork.*

PORK CUTLETS WITH ZESTY SAUCE

SERVES 4

2 ORANGES
2 LEMONS
3 TABLESPOONS FLOUR
½ TEASPOON SALT
½ TEASPOON BLACK PEPPER
8 THIN PORK CUTLETS (ABOUT
   ¾ POUND TOTAL)

2 TABLESPOONS OLIVE OIL
4 SCALLIONS, CUT INTO 2-INCH
   LENGTHS
1 TEASPOON BROWN SUGAR
¾ TEASPOON BASIL
¾ TEASPOON OREGANO

1. Using a sharp knife, cut thin strips of zest from 1 orange and 1 lemon, spacing the strips about ½ inch apart to create a striped effect. Set the strips aside. Cut the orange and lemon crosswise into thin slices. Grate the zest from the remaining orange and lemon. Then juice the orange and measure out ¼ cup of juice. Juice the lemon to get about ¼ cup of juice.

2. In a plastic or paper bag, combine the flour, salt, and pepper, and shake to mix. Add the pork and shake to coat lightly.

3. In a large nonstick skillet, warm 1 tablespoon of the oil over medium-high heat. Add the scallions and reserved strips of orange and lemon zest. Cook, stirring constantly, until

the oil is infused with citrus flavor, 1 to 2 minutes. Transfer the scallions and citrus zest to a plate.

4. Add the remaining 1 tablespoon oil to the pan and warm over medium-high heat. Add the pork cutlets (in batches if necessary) and cook until browned, about 3 minutes per side.

5. Add the orange and lemon juices, the fruit slices, grated zest, brown sugar, basil, oregano, sautéed scallions, and strips of zest, and bring to a boil. Cook until the sauce is slightly thickened and the cutlets are cooked through, about 2 minutes, turning the cutlets over halfway through. Serve hot.

GINGERED PORK CUTLETS

SERVES 4

◆ EXTRA - QUICK

5 QUARTER-SIZE SLICES FRESH
   GINGER—3 SLICES SLIVERED,
   2 SLICES WHOLE

3 GARLIC CLOVES, MINCED

3 TABLESPOONS REDUCED-SODIUM SOY
   SAUCE

2 TABLESPOONS HONEY

1 POUND BONELESS LOIN PORK CHOPS
   (¼ INCH THICK)

2 TABLESPOONS VEGETABLE OIL

4 SCALLIONS, CUT INTO 1½-INCH
   PIECES

1 LARGE RED BELL PEPPER, CUT INTO
   THIN STRIPS

3 TABLESPOONS CORNSTARCH

¼ CUP BEEF BROTH

1. In a shallow bowl, combine the slivered ginger, the garlic, soy sauce, and honey. Add the pork and toss to thoroughly coat.

2. In a large skillet, warm 1 tablespoon of the oil over medium-high heat. Add the 2 whole ginger slices, the scallions, and bell pepper, and stir-fry until the vegetables are just wilted, about 3 minutes. Transfer the vegetables to a plate and set aside.

3. Reserving 3 tablespoons of the marinade, drain the pork. Dredge the pork lightly in the cornstarch, reserving 1 teaspoon of the excess cornstarch.

4. Add the remaining 1 tablespoon oil to the skillet and warm over medium-high heat. Add the pork and cook until browned, about 3 minutes per side.

5. In a cup, combine the reserved 3 tablespoons marinade with the reserved 1 teaspoon cornstarch.

6. Add the cornstarch mixture to the skillet and bring to a boil. Cook, stirring, until the pork is cooked through and the sauce is slightly thickened, about 1 minute. Stir in the broth. Return the vegetables to the pan and cook, stirring, until just heated through, about 1 minute. Serve hot with sauce and the vegetables.

PEPPERED PORK STEAKS WITH PEARS

SERVES 4

1 CUP APPLE JUICE

1 TABLESPOON PLUS 1 TEASPOON FRESH
  LEMON JUICE

2 LARGE BARTLETT PEARS, CUT
  LENGTHWISE INTO THIN SLICES

2 TEASPOONS WHOLE BLACK
  PEPPERCORNS

1 POUND PORK LOIN, CUT INTO
  8 EQUAL SLICES

1 TABLESPOON VEGETABLE OIL

2 TEASPOONS GRATED LEMON ZEST

1 TEASPOON BROWN SUGAR

½ TEASPOON SALT

1. In a medium bowl, combine the apple juice and lemon juice. Add the pears, toss gently to coat, and set aside.

2. Place the peppercorns in a heavy-duty, sealable plastic storage bag. Seal the bag and, with a rolling pin or heavy skillet, press down on the peppercorns to coarsely crush them. Transfer the crushed peppercorns to a sheet of wax paper. Place the pork on top and press to lightly coat with pepper on both sides.

3. In a large nonstick skillet, warm the oil over medium-high heat. Add the pork and cook until lightly browned and cooked through, 3 to 4 minutes per side. Transfer the pork to a plate and cover loosely with foil to keep warm.

4. Add the pears and their liquid, the lemon zest, brown sugar, and salt to the skillet. Bring the mixture to a boil, reduce the heat to medium, and cook until slightly thickened, about 10 minutes.

5. Return the pork (and any juices that have collected on the plate) to the skillet and cook until the pork is heated through, 1 to 2 minutes. With a fork, mash some of the pears in the skillet to thicken the sauce.

6. Serve the pork with the pears and sauce on top.

Red Pepper Pork with Mint

SERVES 4

1 TABLESPOON OLIVE OIL

2 MEDIUM RED BELL PEPPERS, THINLY
  SLICED

1 POUND PORK TENDERLOIN OR LOIN,
  THINLY SLICED

¼ TEASPOON BLACK PEPPER

1 POUND TOMATOES, COARSELY
  CHOPPED

¼ TEASPOON SALT

¼ CUP PLAIN LOW-FAT YOGURT
  (OPTIONAL)

2 TABLESPOONS MINCED FRESH MINT,
  OR ½ TEASPOON DRIED

1. In a large skillet, warm the oil over high heat. Add the bell peppers and cook, stirring frequently, for 1 minute.

2. Add the pork and cook until browned, about 2 minutes per side. Season with ⅛ teaspoon of the black pepper, cover, reduce the heat to medium, and cook for 5 minutes.

3. Stir in the tomatoes, cover, and cook until the pork is tender and the tomato-pepper mixture is reduced, 10 to 15 minutes. Season with the salt and remaining ⅛ teaspoon black pepper.

4. Remove the pork mixture from the heat, let it cool for 1 minute, then stir in the yogurt (if using) and mint. Serve hot.

Kitchen Note: *Red bell peppers can be quite expensive in the winter, when only imported peppers are in the markets. To get the most for your money, choose peppers that look glossy and unblemished, and feel firm to the touch and heavy in your hand. In the late summer, when locally grown peppers are in good supply, try this dish with one of the other colored peppers, such as orange or yellow.*

PORK CHOPS
WITH CARAMELIZED APPLES

SERVES 4

2 TABLESPOONS VEGETABLE OIL

2 TABLESPOONS UNSALTED BUTTER

4 CENTER-CUT LOIN PORK CHOPS
(¾ INCH THICK, ABOUT 2 POUNDS
TOTAL)

¼ CUP DRY WHITE WINE

1¼ CUPS APPLE CIDER OR NATURAL
APPLE JUICE

1 LARGE GOLDEN OR RED DELICIOUS
APPLE

2 TABLESPOONS FRESH LEMON JUICE

1. In a large skillet, warm the oil with 1 table-spoon of the butter over medium-high heat until the butter is melted. Add the pork chops and cook until browned, 2 to 3 minutes per side. Transfer to a plate and set aside.

2. Pour off the excess fat from the pan. Add the wine and bring to a boil over high heat, stirring to scrape up any browned bits cling-ing to the bottom of the pan. Add 1 cup of the cider and cook, stirring constantly, until the liquid is reduced to 1 cup, about 5 min-utes. Remove from the heat.

3. Peel, core, and cut the apple in half lengthwise. With the cut-side down, slice each half into ⅛-inch slices. Place in a medium bowl and sprinkle with the lemon juice to prevent discoloration.

4. Return the chops (and any juices that have collected on the plate) to the pan.

Simmer the chops over low heat until tender, about 10 minutes, turning them over occa-sionally. Transfer the chops to a serving plat-ter and cover loosely with foil to keep warm.

5. Strain the pan juices and reserve in a small bowl. Add the remaining ¼ cup cider and 1 tablespoon butter to the pan and warm over low heat until the butter is melted. Add the apple slices in a single layer, increase the heat to medium-high, and cook, turning the slices occasionally, until the liquid is syrup and the apple slices are caramelized but still hold their shape, about 10 minutes. Spoon the apple slices onto the serving platter with the chops.

6. Return the reserved juices to the pan and cook over medium-high heat until slightly re-duced, 3 to 5 minutes. Spoon over the chops and serve hot.

PORK CHOPS WITH LEMON-SOY SAUCE GLAZE

SERVES 4

◆ EXTRA-QUICK

⅓ CUP REDUCED-SODIUM SOY SAUCE
¼ CUP FRESH LEMON JUICE
¼ CUP BEEF BROTH
2 TABLESPOONS TOMATO PASTE
1 TABLESPOON BROWN SUGAR
2 TEASPOONS GRATED LEMON ZEST
1 TEASPOON GROUND GINGER

¼ TEASPOON BLACK PEPPER
4 CENTER-CUT LOIN PORK CHOPS (½
  INCH THICK, ABOUT 1¼ POUNDS
  TOTAL)
2 TABLESPOONS VEGETABLE OIL
8 SCALLIONS, COARSELY CHOPPED
¼ CUP CORNSTARCH

1. In a small bowl, combine the soy sauce, lemon juice, broth, tomato paste, brown sugar, lemon zest, ginger, and pepper.

2. Place the pork chops in a shallow dish. Pour the lemon-soy mixture over the chops and let them marinate while you cook the scallions.

3. In a large skillet, warm 1 tablespoon of the oil over medium-high heat. Add the scallions and stir-fry until they are just limp, about 3 minutes. Transfer to a plate and set aside.

4. Reserving the marinade, remove the pork chops from the marinade. Dredge the chops in the cornstarch, shaking off the excess.

5. Add the remaining 1 tablespoon oil to the skillet and warm over medium-high heat. Add the pork chops and cook until golden, about 3 minutes per side.

6. Add the reserved marinade to the skillet and bring to a boil, turning the chops once. Simmer the pork chops until cooked through, about 8 minutes. Return the scallions to the pan and stir to blend.

7. Serve the pork chops with the scallions and sauce spooned on top.

GERMAN-STYLE
PORK CHOPS WITH MUSHROOMS

SERVES 4

¼ CUP FLOUR

1½ TEASPOONS THYME

½ TEASPOON SALT

¼ TEASPOON BLACK PEPPER

4 CENTER-CUT LOIN PORK CHOPS
(½ INCH THICK, ABOUT 1¼ POUNDS
TOTAL)

1 TABLESPOON OLIVE OIL

2 GARLIC CLOVES, MINCED

1 MEDIUM ONION, COARSELY CHOPPED

½ POUND MUSHROOMS, QUARTERED

½ CUP DARK BEER

½ CUP CHICKEN BROTH

1. In a plastic or paper bag, combine the flour, ½ teaspoon of the thyme, the salt, and pepper, and shake to mix. Add the pork chops and shake to coat lightly. Remove the chops and reserve 1 tablespoon of the excess seasoned flour.

2. In a large skillet, warm the oil over medium-high heat. Add the pork chops and cook until well browned, about 5 minutes per side. Transfer the pork chops to a plate and cover loosely with foil to keep warm.

3. Add the garlic, onion, and mushrooms to the skillet and cook, stirring frequently, over medium-high heat for 1 minute. Add the 1 ta-

blespoon reserved seasoned flour and cook, stirring constantly, until the flour is no longer visible, about 1 minute.

4. Stir in the beer, broth, and remaining 1 teaspoon thyme, and bring to a boil. Return the pork chops (and any juices that have collected on the plate) to the skillet and return to a boil. Reduce the heat to low, cover, and simmer until the chops are cooked through, about 8 minutes, turning the chops over halfway through.

5. Uncover the skillet and cook until the sauce has thickened slightly, about 2 minutes. Serve the chops hot, with mushrooms on top.

PORK CHOPS WITH APPLES AND ONIONS

SERVES 4

3 TABLESPOONS VEGETABLE OIL

2 MEDIUM ONIONS, CUT INTO ½-INCH WEDGES

1 UNPEELED GRANNY SMITH APPLE, CUT INTO ¼-INCH WEDGES

¼ CUP FLOUR

½ TEASPOON SALT

¼ TEASPOON BLACK PEPPER

4 CENTER-CUT LOIN PORK CHOPS (¾ INCH THICK, ABOUT 2 POUNDS TOTAL)

½ CUP BEEF BROTH

2 TABLESPOONS THAWED FROZEN APPLE JUICE CONCENTRATE

1 TABLESPOON DIJON MUSTARD

1. In a large skillet, warm 1 tablespoon of the oil over medium-high heat. Add the onions and apple, and cook, stirring frequently, until the mixture begins to brown, 2 to 3 minutes. Transfer the onions and apple to a plate and set aside.

2. In a shallow bowl, combine the flour, salt, and pepper. Dredge the pork chops lightly in the seasoned flour, shaking off the excess.

3. Add the remaining 2 tablespoons oil to the skillet and warm over medium-high heat. Add the pork chops and cook until golden, about 4 minutes per side.

4. Add the broth, apple juice concentrate, and mustard, and bring to a boil. Reduce the heat to medium-low, cover, and simmer for 10 minutes.

5. Turn the pork chops over. Return the sautéed onions and apple to the pan, cover, and simmer until the pork chops are cooked through, about 10 minutes.

6. Serve the pork chops topped with some of the onions and apple.

PORK CHOPS DIABLO

SERVES 4

◆ EXTRA-QUICK

⅓ CUP FLOUR

2 TABLESPOONS CHILI POWDER

¼ TEASPOON BLACK PEPPER

PINCH OF CAYENNE PEPPER

4 SMALL CENTER-CUT LOIN PORK
CHOPS (½ INCH THICK, ABOUT ¾
POUND TOTAL)

2 TEASPOONS VEGETABLE OIL

1 TABLESPOON UNSALTED BUTTER

1 LARGE ONION, CUT INTO THIN
WEDGES

ONE 8-OUNCE CAN TOMATO SAUCE

⅓ CUP BEEF BROTH

2 TEASPOONS WORCESTERSHIRE SAUCE

4 TO 5 DROPS OF HOT PEPPER SAUCE,
TO TASTE

1 TEASPOON DRY MUSTARD

1. In a plastic or paper bag, combine the flour, chili powder, black pepper, and cayenne, and shake to mix. Add the pork chops and shake to coat lightly. Remove the chops and reserve 1 tablespoon of the excess seasoned flour.

2. In a large skillet, warm the oil over medium-high heat. Add the pork chops and cook until browned, about 3 minutes per side. Transfer the chops to a plate and cover loosely with foil to keep warm.

3. Add the butter and the onion to the skillet and cook, stirring frequently, until the onion begins to brown, about 3 minutes.

4. Stir in the reserved 1 tablespoon seasoned flour and cook, stirring constantly, until the flour is no longer visible, about 30 seconds. Add the tomato sauce, broth, Worcestershire sauce, hot pepper sauce, and mustard.

5. Pour any juices that have collected under the chops into the skillet and bring the mixture to a boil over medium-high heat, stirring constantly. Add the chops, reduce the heat to low, cover, and simmer until the chops are cooked through, about 12 minutes, turning the chops over halfway through.

6. Serve the chops topped with the sauce and onions.

PORK CHOPS
WITH ORANGE SAUCE

SERVES 4

1 TABLESPOON OLIVE OIL

4 LOIN PORK CHOPS (1 INCH THICK,
ABOUT 2 POUNDS TOTAL)

¾ CUP ORANGE JUICE

1 TEASPOON SUGAR

1 TEASPOON WHOLE CLOVES

½ TEASPOON SALT

½ TEASPOON CORNSTARCH BLENDED
WITH 2 TABLESPOONS WATER

1 MEDIUM NAVEL ORANGE, PEELED
AND SLICED

1. In a large skillet, warm the oil over medium-high heat. Add the chops and cook until browned, about 4 minutes per side.

2. Add the orange juice, sugar, cloves, and salt to the pan, increase the heat to high, and bring to a boil. Reduce the heat to low, cover, and simmer until the chops are tender, about 25 minutes. Transfer the chops to a plate and cover loosely with foil to keep warm.

3. Boil the liquid in the pan over high heat until reduced by half, about 10 minutes.

4. Whisk the cornstarch mixture into the boiling liquid. Cook, whisking constantly, until the sauce is thickened, about 1 minute. Remove and discard the cloves.

5. Divide the pork chops among 4 dinner plates, top with the sauce, and garnish with the orange slices.

SWEET AFTERTHOUGHT: *Soften a pint of vanilla ice cream (microwave it in the container for 30 seconds at Medium-Low power), then stir in 2 tablespoons of finely chopped crystallized ginger and 3 tablespoons of miniature chocolate chips. Return the ice cream to the freezer until it's time for dessert.*

PORK WITH APPLE-CARAWAY CREAM

SERVES 4

◆ EXTRA-QUICK

- 4 BONELESS PORK CHOPS (ABOUT ¾ POUND TOTAL)
- 2 TABLESPOONS FLOUR
- 1 TABLESPOON VEGETABLE OIL
- 2 MEDIUM ONIONS, CUT INTO THIN WEDGES
- 3 GARLIC CLOVES, MINCED
- 1 TABLESPOON UNSALTED BUTTER
- ¼ CUP DRY WHITE WINE

- ¼ CUP BEEF BROTH
- 1 TABLESPOON DIJON MUSTARD
- 1 TEASPOON CARAWAY SEEDS
- ½ TEASPOON SALT
- ¼ TEASPOON BLACK PEPPER
- ¼ TEASPOON DRY MUSTARD
- 1 UNPEELED RED APPLE, CUT INTO THIN WEDGES
- ¼ CUP REDUCED-FAT SOUR CREAM

1. Lightly dredge the pork in the flour, reserving the excess flour.

2. In a large nonstick skillet, warm 2 teaspoons of the oil over medium-high heat. Add the onions and garlic, and cook, stirring frequently, until the onions begin to brown, 3 to 5 minutes. Transfer the onions to a plate.

3. Add the remaining 1 teaspoon oil to the skillet and warm over medium-high heat. Add the pork and cook until browned, about 3 minutes per side. Transfer the pork to the plate with the onions and cover loosely with foil to keep warm.

4. Add the butter to the skillet and warm until melted. Add the reserved flour and cook, stirring, until the flour is no longer visible, about 30 seconds. Stir in the wine, broth, Dijon mustard, caraway seeds, salt, pepper, and dry mustard.

5. Bring the mixture to a boil and add the apple. Return the pork and onions (and any juices that have collected on the plate) to the pan, reduce the heat to low, cover, and simmer until the pork is cooked through, about 7 minutes, turning the pork over halfway through.

6. Transfer the pork to 4 plates. Stir the sour cream into the sauce and spoon the apples and sauce over the pork.

Sautéed Sausage, Mushrooms, and Peppers

SERVES 4

1½ POUNDS SWEET ITALIAN SAUSAGE,
   CASINGS REMOVED
1 TABLESPOON OLIVE OIL
1 TABLESPOON UNSALTED BUTTER
¾ POUND MUSHROOMS, THINLY SLICED
1 SMALL RED BELL PEPPER, DICED
3 TABLESPOONS CHOPPED PARSLEY

1 TABLESPOON CHOPPED FRESH MINT,
   OR 1 TEASPOON DRIED
1½ TEASPOONS MINCED FRESH THYME,
   OR ½ TEASPOON DRIED
1 TEASPOON BASIL
½ TEASPOON SALT
⅛ TEASPOON BLACK PEPPER

1. In a large skillet, cook the sausage over low heat, stirring frequently to break up the meat, for 2 minutes. Cover the pan and cook until the meat is no longer pink, about 10 minutes.

2. Uncover the pan and drain off all the fat. Increase the heat to medium and cook the sausage, stirring to break up any large clumps, until evenly browned, about 5 minutes. Transfer the sausage to a medium bowl and cover loosely with foil to keep warm.

3. In the same skillet, warm the oil with the butter over medium heat until the butter is melted. Increase the heat to high and add the mushrooms. Sauté, stirring constantly, until the liquid has evaporated and the mushrooms have begun to brown, about 5 minutes.

4. Stir in the sausage, bell pepper, parsley, mint, thyme, and basil, and cook, stirring constantly, for 1 minute. Stir in the salt and black pepper, and serve hot.

Ham Steak with Maple-Bourbon Glaze

SERVES 4 TO 6

1½ TABLESPOONS UNSALTED BUTTER

2½ POUNDS CENTER-CUT HAM STEAK
(ABOUT 1½ INCHES THICK)

1 TEASPOON FLOUR

¼ TEASPOON DRY MUSTARD

PINCH OF GROUND CLOVES

¼ CUP PLUS 2 TABLESPOONS DRY RED
WINE

¼ CUP PURE MAPLE SYRUP

2 TABLESPOONS BOURBON

1. In a large skillet, warm the butter over medium heat until melted. Add the ham and cook until well browned, about 7 minutes per side. Transfer the ham to a plate and cover loosely with foil to keep warm. Set the skillet aside to cool slightly.

2. Meanwhile, in a small bowl, combine the flour, mustard, and cloves. Add 2 tablespoons of water and stir until the mixture is smooth.

3. Return the skillet to low heat. Add the flour mixture, wine, maple syrup, and bourbon, and stir until blended. Cook, stirring constantly, until the mixture begins to thicken to a glaze consistency, 1 to 2 minutes.

4. Return the ham to the pan, spooning the glaze on top, and cook until heated through, turning once or twice, about 8 minutes.

5. Transfer the ham to a cutting board and cut into thin slices. Serve the ham topped with the glaze.

Kitchen Note: *The deep, distinctive flavor of real maple syrup serves as a perfect counterpoint to the smoky ham. The recipe is not nearly as tasty if you try to make the sauce with pancake syrup, which is just corn syrup doctored up with a bit of flavoring.*

BEEF TOSSED WITH RED CABBAGE AND APPLES

SERVES 6

◇ LOW-FAT

2 CUPS DRY RED WINE

1 CUP BEEF OR CHICKEN BROTH, PREFERABLY REDUCED-SODIUM

¼ CUP CHOPPED SHALLOTS OR ONION

2 TEASPOONS CARAWAY SEEDS

¼ TEASPOON SALT

1 SMALL RED CABBAGE, QUARTERED AND THINLY SLICED

2 UNPEELED GRANNY SMITH APPLES, CUT INTO ¼-INCH-WIDE WEDGES

¼ CUP FRESH LEMON JUICE

1 TABLESPOON HONEY

1¾ POUNDS SIRLOIN STEAK, CUT INTO THIN STRIPS ABOUT 1½ INCHES LONG

1 TEASPOON BLACK PEPPER

1½ TABLESPOONS VEGETABLE OIL

2 SCALLIONS, SLICED

1. In a medium saucepan, combine the wine, broth, shallots, 1 teaspoon of the caraway seeds, and the salt. Cook over medium heat until the liquid is reduced to ½ cup, about 40 minutes.

2. Meanwhile, in a large bowl, combine the cabbage, apples, and the remaining 1 teaspoon caraway seeds. In a cup, mix the lemon juice and honey, pour it over the cabbage mixture, and toss well to combine. Set aside.

3. Place the beef in a medium bowl and sprinkle it with the pepper. Pour the reduced wine mixture over the beef and stir well.

4. In a large skillet, warm 1 tablespoon of the oil over high heat. Add the beef with its liquid and the scallions, and stir-fry until the meat is browned, about 1½ minutes. Transfer the mixture to a bowl.

5. In the same skillet, warm the remaining 1½ teaspoons oil over medium-high heat. Add the cabbage-apple mixture and stir-fry until the cabbage has wilted slightly, 3 to 4 minutes. Return the beef mixture to the skillet, toss well, and serve hot.

Beef and Mushroom Stir-Fry

SERVES 4

♦ EXTRA-QUICK

¾ POUND FLANK STEAK, CUT WITH THE GRAIN INTO 2 STRIPS, THEN ACROSS THE GRAIN INTO THIN SLICES

2 TABLESPOONS REDUCED-SODIUM SOY SAUCE

1 TABLESPOON CORNSTARCH

⅓ CUP BEEF BROTH

3 DROPS OF HOT PEPPER SAUCE

¼ TEASPOON BLACK PEPPER

2 TABLESPOONS VEGETABLE OIL

8 SCALLIONS, CUT INTO 2-INCH LENGTHS

3 QUARTER-SIZE SLICES FRESH GINGER

2 GARLIC CLOVES, MINCED

4 LARGE CARROTS, THINLY SLICED ON THE DIAGONAL

½ POUND SMALL MUSHROOMS, HALVED OR QUARTERED IF LARGE

3 TABLESPOONS CHOPPED CILANTRO (OPTIONAL)

1. In a medium bowl, combine the steak, 1 tablespoon of the soy sauce, and the cornstarch. Stir to coat the steak and set aside.

2. In a small bowl, combine the broth, remaining 1 tablespoon soy sauce, the hot pepper sauce, and black pepper. Set aside.

3. In a large skillet or wok, warm 1 tablespoon of the oil over medium-high heat. Add the scallions, ginger, and garlic, and stir-fry for 30 seconds. Add the carrots and mushrooms, and stir-fry until the carrots are crisp-tender, 3 to 5 minutes. Transfer to a plate and cover loosely with foil to keep warm.

4. Add the remaining 1 tablespoon oil to the skillet and warm over medium-high heat. Add the steak and its marinade and stir-fry until the steak is browned but still slightly pink in the center, 2 to 3 minutes.

5. Return the vegetables to the skillet. Stir the broth mixture, add it to the skillet, and bring the liquid to a boil. Cook, stirring constantly, until the vegetables are tender and the beef is cooked through, 2 to 3 minutes. Stir in the cilantro (if using) and serve hot.

GINGER ORANGE BEEF

SERVES 4

◆ EXTRA-QUICK

1 TABLESPOON CORNSTARCH

1 TABLESPOON REDUCED-SODIUM SOY
SAUCE

2 DROPS OF HOT PEPPER SAUCE

¼ POUND FLANK STEAK, CUT WITH THE
GRAIN INTO 2 STRIPS, THEN ACROSS
THE GRAIN INTO THIN SLICES

1 TABLESPOON VEGETABLE OIL

⅔ CUP BEEF BROTH

2 GARLIC CLOVES, MINCED

3 QUARTER-SIZE SLICES FRESH GINGER,
MINCED

1 TABLESPOON GRATED ORANGE ZEST

½ POUND FRESH GREEN BEANS, CUT
INTO 2-INCH LENGTHS, OR ONE
10-OUNCE PACKAGE FROZEN CUT
GREEN BEANS, THAWED

2 MEDIUM CARROTS, THINLY SLICED

2 SCALLIONS, COARSELY CHOPPED

ONE 8-OUNCE CAN SLICED WATER
CHESTNUTS, DRAINED

1. In a medium bowl, combine 1 teaspoon of the cornstarch, the soy sauce, and hot pepper sauce. Add the steak strips and toss to coat.

2. In a large nonstick skillet or wok, warm the oil over medium-high heat. Add the steak strips and stir-fry until the meat is browned but still slightly pink inside. Transfer the meat to a plate and cover loosely with foil to keep warm.

3. Add the broth, garlic, ginger, and orange zest to the skillet and bring to a boil over medium-high heat. Add the green beans, carrots, scallions, and water chestnuts. Return

the mixture to a boil. Reduce the heat to medium-low, cover, and cook for 4 minutes.

4. Meanwhile, in a small bowl, combine the remaining 2 teaspoons cornstarch with 1 tablespoon of water, and stir to blend.

5. Bring the vegetable mixture back to a boil over medium-high heat and stir in the cornstarch mixture. Return the steak strips (and any juices that have collected on the plate) to the skillet and cook, stirring constantly, until the meat is cooked through and the sauce is slightly thickened, about 4 minutes.

Stir-Fried Flank Steak and Vegetables

SERVES 4 TO 6

◆ EXTRA-QUICK

3 TABLESPOONS VEGETABLE OIL

1½ POUNDS FLANK STEAK, CUT WITH
THE GRAIN INTO 2 STRIPS, THEN
ACROSS THE GRAIN INTO THIN
SLICES

3 CUPS BROCCOLI FLORETS

10 CHERRY TOMATOES, HALVED

3 LARGE CARROTS, THINLY SLICED ON
THE DIAGONAL

2 TABLESPOONS MINCED FRESH GINGER

¼ CUP REDUCED-SODIUM SOY SAUCE

1. Warm a wok or Dutch oven over high heat. Add the oil and tilt and rotate the pan to coat the sides. When the oil is hot enough to evaporate a drop of water on contact, add the steak and stir-fry until it is lightly browned, 2 to 3 minutes.

2. Add the broccoli, tomatoes, and carrots, and stir-fry for 3 minutes. Reduce the heat to medium, add the ginger and soy sauce, and toss to combine. Cover the pan and cook for 1 minute.

3. Divide the steak and vegetables among 4 dinner plates and serve hot.

Variation: *Stir-fries are wonderfully flexible. You can vary this one with different seasonal vegetables, always giving some thought to color and texture so the dish retains its fresh appeal. Experiment with asparagus, snow peas, yellow snap beans, cauliflower, and the various Chinese cabbages, including bok choy and napa. Use a total of about 7 cups of vegetables, making sure that you cut them on the small side so they will cook quickly.*

Top Round Sautéed with Broccoli and Cauliflower

SERVES 4 TO 6

1½ POUNDS BEEF TOP ROUND STEAK, CUT INTO VERY THIN STRIPS ABOUT 1½ INCHES LONG

½ TEASPOON RED PEPPER FLAKES

4 GARLIC CLOVES, MINCED

1 POUND BROCCOLI—STALKS PEELED AND CUT INTO THIN STRIPS ABOUT 1½ INCHES LONG, THE TOPS CUT INTO SMALL FLORETS

½ LARGE HEAD OF CAULIFLOWER, CUT INTO SMALL FLORETS

1½ CUPS BEEF OR CHICKEN BROTH, PREFERABLY REDUCED-SODIUM

1 TABLESPOON CORNSTARCH

2 TABLESPOONS VEGETABLE OIL

½ TEASPOON SALT

2 LEMONS, PEELED AND VERY COARSELY CHOPPED

1. In a medium bowl, combine the steak strips, red pepper flakes, and garlic, and set aside while you prepare the other ingredients.

2. In a large pot of boiling water, blanch the broccoli and cauliflower together for 1 minute. Drain the vegetables and rinse them under cold running water.

3. In a small saucepan, boil the broth over high heat until it is reduced to about ⅔ cup. In a small bowl, combine 2 tablespoons of the reduced broth with the cornstarch, and stir to blend. Set the broth and the cornstarch mixture aside.

4. In a large nonstick skillet or wok, warm 1 tablespoon of the oil over high heat. Add the broccoli and cauliflower, sprinkle them with the salt, and stir-fry for 2 minutes. Transfer the vegetables to a plate.

5. Add the remaining 1 tablespoon oil to the skillet and warm over medium-high heat. Add the steak strips and stir-fry until they are lightly browned, about 1 minute.

6. Return the broccoli and cauliflower to the skillet. Pour in the broth and the cornstarch mixture, then add half the lemon pieces. Stir-fry the mixture for 1½ minutes and, with a slotted spoon, transfer it to a serving dish. Boil the sauce remaining in the pan until it is reduced to about ½ cup, and pour it over the meat and vegetables. Scatter the remaining lemon pieces over the top and serve hot.

Hawaiian Pork Skillet

SERVES 4

♦ EXTRA-QUICK

1 POUND BONELESS PORK LOIN

ONE 8-OUNCE CAN JUICE-PACKED
   PINEAPPLE CHUNKS

3 TABLESPOONS REDUCED-SODIUM SOY
   SAUCE

1 TABLESPOON CORNSTARCH

1 TABLESPOON VEGETABLE OIL

1 TABLESPOON ORIENTAL (DARK)
   SESAME OIL

4 QUARTER-SIZE SLICES FRESH GINGER,
   MINCED

2 GARLIC CLOVES, MINCED

1 LARGE RED BELL PEPPER, SLIVERED

4 SCALLIONS, COARSELY CHOPPED

¼ TEASPOON BLACK PEPPER

1. Cut the pork loin with the grain into 4 strips, then cut across the grain into ¼-inch-thick slices.

2. Drain the pineapple, reserving the juice. In a medium bowl, combine the pineapple juice and soy sauce. Add the pork slices, toss to coat, and let the pork marinate for about 10 minutes. Set the pineapple chunks aside.

3. Remove the pork from the pineapple-soy mixture, reserving the liquid. On a sheet of wax paper, toss the pork with the cornstarch (the pork will be somewhat gummy).

4. In a large skillet or wok, warm the vegetable and sesame oils over medium-high heat. Add the ginger and garlic, and stir-fry for 1 minute. Add the pork and stir-fry until well browned, about 6 minutes.

5. Add the bell pepper, scallions, black pepper, and reserved pineapple-soy marinade, and bring to a boil. Cook, stirring, until the sauce thickens slightly and the bell pepper begins to soften, about 2 minutes.

6. Add the pineapple chunks and cook, stirring, until they are heated through, 1 to 2 minutes. Serve hot.

ORANGE PORK STIR-FRY

SERVES 4

◆ EXTRA-QUICK

1 POUND BONELESS PORK LOIN, CUT
WITH THE GRAIN INTO 2 STRIPS,
THEN ACROSS THE GRAIN INTO
THIN SLICES

3 TABLESPOONS PEANUT OR OTHER
VEGETABLE OIL

2 TABLESPOONS REDUCED-SODIUM SOY
SAUCE

1 TABLESPOON PLUS 2 TEASPOONS
CORNSTARCH

¾ CUP BEEF BROTH

2 TABLESPOONS KETCHUP

1 TEASPOON GRATED ORANGE ZEST
(OPTIONAL)

8 SCALLIONS, CUT INTO 2-INCH
LENGTHS

3 QUARTER-SIZE SLICES FRESH GINGER

1 LARGE GREEN BELL PEPPER, CUT INTO
1-INCH SQUARES

ONE 11-OUNCE CAN MANDARIN
ORANGES, DRAINED

1. In a medium bowl, combine the pork with 1 tablespoon each of the oil, soy sauce, and cornstarch. Mix gently until the pork is well coated.

2. In a small bowl, stir together the broth, ketchup, orange zest (if using), and the remaining 1 tablespoon soy sauce and 2 teaspoons cornstarch. Set aside.

3. In a large skillet or wok, warm 1 tablespoon of the oil over medium-high heat. Add the pork and its marinade and stir-fry until the pork is browned but still slightly pink in the center, 3 to 4 minutes. Transfer the pork to a plate and set aside.

4. Add the remaining 1 tablespoon oil to the skillet. Add the scallions, ginger, and bell pepper, and stir-fry until the scallions wilt, 3 to 4 minutes. Return the pork to the skillet. Stir the broth mixture, then stir it into the skillet. Bring the liquid to a boil.

5. Add the oranges and cook, stirring constantly, until the vegetables are crisp-tender and the pork is cooked through, 2 to 3 minutes. Discard the ginger slices before serving.

STIR-FRIED LAMB WITH GREEN BEANS

SERVES 4

◆ EXTRA-QUICK

1 CUP BEEF OR CHICKEN BROTH,
   PREFERABLY REDUCED-SODIUM
3 TABLESPOONS MINCED SHALLOT OR
   ONION
2 TABLESPOONS BRANDY
1½ TABLESPOONS RICE WINE VINEGAR
2 TEASPOONS REDUCED-SODIUM SOY
   SAUCE
¼ TEASPOON SALT

½ POUND GREEN BEANS, HALVED ON
   THE DIAGONAL
1½ TABLESPOONS VEGETABLE OIL
4 GARLIC CLOVES, MINCED
1 TEASPOON RED PEPPER FLAKES
2 TEASPOONS MINCED FRESH GINGER
1¼ POUNDS LEAN BONELESS LAMB (LEG
   OR LOIN), CUT INTO THIN STRIPS

1. In a small saucepan, bring the broth to a simmer over medium heat. Add the shallot, brandy, vinegar, soy sauce, and salt, and simmer the mixture until it is reduced to about ¼ cup, 15 to 20 minutes.

2. Meanwhile, in a vegetable steamer, steam the green beans until just crisp-tender, about 3 minutes. Transfer the beans to a colander and rinse under cold running water. Set aside.

3. In a large nonstick skillet or wok, warm the oil over high heat. Add the garlic, red pepper flakes, and ginger, and stir-fry for 1 minute. Add the green beans and lamb, and stir-fry until the meat is browned, about 2 minutes.

4. Pour the reduced broth mixture over the lamb and green beans, stir well, and stir-fry the mixture until it is well coated, about 30 seconds. Serve hot.

SPICY LAMB SAUTÉ

SERVES 4

◆ EXTRA-QUICK ◇ LOW-FAT

½ POUND BOW TIE PASTA

1 POUND LEAN BONELESS LAMB (LEG OR LOIN), CUT WITH THE GRAIN INTO 2 STRIPS, THEN ACROSS THE GRAIN INTO THIN SLICES

¼ CUP CORNSTARCH

2 TABLESPOONS OLIVE OIL

3 QUARTER-SIZE SLICES FRESH GINGER, MINCED

3 GARLIC CLOVES, MINCED

1 LARGE RED BELL PEPPER, CUT INTO ¾-INCH SQUARES

ONE 10-OUNCE PACKAGE FROZEN GREEN BEANS, THAWED

⅔ CUP BEEF BROTH

2 TABLESPOONS REDUCED-SODIUM SOY SAUCE

1 TABLESPOON RED WINE VINEGAR OR CIDER VINEGAR

½ TEASPOON SUGAR

¼ TEASPOON RED PEPPER FLAKES

1. In a large pot of boiling water, cook the pasta until al dente according to package directions.

2. Meanwhile, in a medium bowl, toss the lamb strips with 2 tablespoons of the cornstarch until evenly coated.

3. In a large skillet or wok, warm 1 tablespoon of the oil over medium-high heat. Add the lamb and stir-fry until lightly browned, about 4 minutes. Transfer the lamb to a plate and cover loosely with foil to keep warm.

4. Add the remaining 1 tablespoon oil to the skillet. Add the ginger and garlic, and stir-fry until the garlic begins to brown, 1 to 2 min-

utes. Add the bell pepper, green beans, ⅓ cup of the broth, the soy sauce, vinegar, sugar, and red pepper flakes, and bring to a boil.

5. Meanwhile, in a cup, combine the remaining ⅓ cup broth and 2 tablespoons cornstarch. Add the lamb (and any juices that have collected on the plate) to the boiling vegetable mixture. Add the cornstarch mixture and cook, stirring constantly, until the mixture has thickened, 2 to 3 minutes.

6. Drain the pasta and serve topped with the lamb mixture.

Oven-Roasted
Steak Kebabs with Potatoes

SERVES 4

4 TABLESPOONS UNSALTED BUTTER

1 POUND SMALL UNPEELED RED
   POTATOES, QUARTERED

¼ CUP DRY RED WINE OR BEEF BROTH

2 TABLESPOONS DIJON MUSTARD

1 TABLESPOON OLIVE OIL

1 TABLESPOON MINCED FRESH
   TARRAGON, OR 1 TEASPOON DRIED

½ TEASPOON DRY MUSTARD

1 GARLIC CLOVE, MINCED

¼ TEASPOON BLACK PEPPER

1 POUND SIRLOIN STEAK, CUT INTO
   1½-INCH CUBES

8 SCALLIONS, CUT INTO 1½-INCH
   LENGTHS

1. Preheat the oven to 425°. Line a broiler pan with foil.

2. In a small skillet, warm 2 tablespoons of the butter over medium heat until melted. Remove from the heat.

3. Place the potatoes on the broiler pan, drizzle the melted butter over them, and toss to coat evenly. Roast the potatoes in the oven for 20 minutes, or until just beginning to brown. Remove them from the oven and set aside. Preheat the broiler.

4. Meanwhile, in a small saucepan, combine the wine, Dijon mustard, oil, tarragon, dry mustard, garlic, and pepper, and stir to blend.

5. Alternately thread the steak cubes and scallion pieces onto skewers. Move the pota-toes to one side of the broiler pan and place the skewers on the pan. Brush the steak and scallions with some of the tarragon-mustard mixture and broil 4 inches from the heat for 5 minutes. Turn the kebabs over, brush with a little more tarragon-mustard mixture, and broil for 7 minutes, or until the meat is medium-rare.

6. Meanwhile, bring the remaining tarragon-mustard mixture to a boil over medium heat. Reduce the heat to low and simmer for 10 minutes. Stir in the remaining 2 tablespoons butter. Remove from the heat.

7. Divide the steak kebabs among 4 plates and pour any pan juices from the broiler pan into the sauce. Serve the kebabs with the sauce and potatoes on the side.

Pecan-Mustard Pork Chops

SERVES 4

⅓ CUP GRAINY MUSTARD

¼ CUP DIJON MUSTARD

¼ CUP DRY WHITE WINE

1 CUP PECANS, FINELY CHOPPED

1 SLICE FIRM-TEXTURED BREAD, TORN
INTO FINE CRUMBS

3 TABLESPOONS MINCED PARSLEY

1½ TEASPOONS MINCED GARLIC

¼ CUP OLIVE OIL

8 SMALL LOIN PORK CHOPS (½ INCH
THICK, ABOUT 2½ POUNDS TOTAL)

¼ TEASPOON BLACK PEPPER

1 TABLESPOON UNSALTED BUTTER,
MELTED

1. Preheat the oven to 375°.

2. In a shallow bowl, combine the mustards with the wine, and stir to blend. In another shallow bowl, combine the pecans, bread crumbs, parsley, and garlic.

3. In a large skillet, warm 2 tablespoons of the oil over medium-high heat. Sprinkle the chops with the pepper. Add 4 chops to the pan and sear for 1 to 2 minutes per side. With tongs, dip the chops one at a time into the mustard-wine mixture, coating both sides.

Then place each chop in the pecan-crumb mixture to coat, pressing the crumbs into the chops to make them adhere. Place the chops in a single layer in a large baking pan.

4. In the same skillet, warm the remaining 2 tablespoons oil and repeat with the remaining chops and coating mixtures.

5. Drizzle the chops with the melted butter and bake them for 20 minutes, or until a crust forms on top and the pork chops are cooked through. Serve hot.

KITCHEN NOTE: *Nuts, because of their high fat content, are very perishable. Both shelled and unshelled nuts should be stored in air-tight containers in the freezer. Shelled nuts will keep for six months or so, unshelled nuts for up to twice that long.*

Roasted Pork Loin Provençale

SERVES 6

2½ to 2¾ pounds pork loin—
   boned, rolled, and tied
⅓ cup plus 2 tablespoons fresh
   lemon juice
1 tablespoon sage
¼ teaspoon salt
¼ teaspoon black pepper
4 garlic cloves, slivered, plus
   6 garlic cloves, peeled

⅔ cup olive oil
½ pound oil-cured black olives,
   pitted and slivered
½ cup chopped fresh basil
3 tablespoons capers, rinsed and
   drained
6 anchovy fillets, rinsed and
   drained
1 loaf of French bread, sliced

1. Preheat the oven to 475°.

2. Rub the pork with 2 tablespoons of the lemon juice, then sprinkle it with the sage, salt, and pepper, lightly patting the seasonings into the meat. Arrange the slivered garlic on top of the pork in 2 lengthwise rows.

3. Place the pork on a rack in a roasting pan and roast for 10 minutes. Lower the oven temperature to 375°, and roast for 40 to 50 minutes, or until a meat thermometer registers 155°. Let the pork rest for 10 minutes before slicing.

4. Meanwhile, in a food processor or blender, combine the oil, olives, basil, capers, anchovies, the peeled garlic, and the remaining ⅓ cup lemon juice. Purée the mixture until it is thick and smooth.

5. Cut the pork into thin slices and serve it with the olive spread and bread slices.

BULGUR-STUFFED RED PEPPERS

SERVES 4

◇ LOW-FAT

4 LARGE RED OR GREEN BELL PEPPERS
1 TABLESPOON PLUS 1 TEASPOON OLIVE
   OIL
¼ POUND MUSHROOMS, THINLY SLICED
¾ CUP BULGUR
2 TABLESPOONS FINELY CHOPPED
   CELERY
1 MEDIUM ONION, CHOPPED
½ TEASPOON THYME

¼ TEASPOON SALT
¼ TEASPOON BLACK PEPPER
1½ CUPS BEEF OR CHICKEN BROTH,
   PREFERABLY REDUCED-SODIUM
¾ POUND LEAN GROUND ROUND
1 GARLIC CLOVE, MINCED
2 TABLESPOONS SHERRY VINEGAR OR
   RED WINE VINEGAR

1. Preheat the oven to 400°.

2. Slice the tops off the bell peppers, chop, and set aside. Remove the ribs and seeds from the peppers. Set the peppers aside.

3. In a medium saucepan, warm 1 tablespoon of the oil over medium heat. Add the mushrooms, bulgur, celery, half of the onion, ¼ teaspoon of the thyme, and ⅛ teaspoon each of the salt and black pepper, and cook, stirring frequently, for 5 minutes.

4. Add the broth, stir the mixture well, and cover the pan. Cook the mixture, stirring occasionally, until the liquid is absorbed, about 12 minutes.

5. Meanwhile, in a large nonstick skillet, warm the remaining 1 teaspoon oil over

medium-high heat. Add the beef, the reserved chopped peppers, the remaining onion, the remaining ¼ teaspoon thyme, and the garlic. Cook, stirring frequently, until the beef is browned, 5 to 7 minutes. Stir in the vinegar and the remaining ⅛ teaspoon each salt and black pepper. Cook the mixture for 30 seconds, then remove it from the heat.

6. Combine the bulgur mixture with the beef mixture. Divide the stuffing mixture among the bell peppers, mounding the filling. Transfer the peppers to a shallow casserole, cover loosely with foil, and bake for 25 minutes, or until the filling is hot. Let the stuffed peppers stand for 5 minutes before serving.

HAM AND
SWISS CHEESE CASSEROLES

SERVES 4

1½ POUNDS SMALL UNPEELED RED
   POTATOES, CUT INTO ½-INCH
   SLICES
2 CUPS BROCCOLI FLORETS
2 TABLESPOONS UNSALTED BUTTER
2 TABLESPOONS FLOUR
1¼ CUPS MILK
¼ TEASPOON SALT

⅛ TEASPOON BLACK PEPPER
PINCH OF NUTMEG
½ POUND SWISS OR GRUYÈRE
   CHEESE—2 CUPS CUBED AND THE
   REMAINDER CUT INTO THIN STRIPS
¾ POUND BLACK FOREST OR OTHER
   SMOKED HAM, IN ONE PIECE, CUT
   INTO 1-INCH CUBES

1. In a large pot of boiling water, cook the potatoes for 8 minutes. Add the broccoli to the pot and cook the potatoes and broccoli for 5 minutes, or until the vegetables are tender. Drain well and set aside.

2. Meanwhile, preheat the oven to 400°. Grease 4 individual heatproof casseroles.

3. In a small saucepan, warm the butter over medium heat until melted. Stir in the flour until well combined. Gradually add the milk and cook, stirring constantly, until the mixture is smooth, about 1 minute. Add the salt, pepper, and nutmeg, and cook, stirring occa-sionally, until the mixture just comes to a boil, about 4 minutes. Remove from the heat and stir in the cheese cubes.

4. Divide half of the potatoes, broccoli, and ham among the prepared casseroles. Spoon about ¼ cup of the cheese sauce into each casserole and top with the remaining vegetables and ham. Spoon the remaining sauce on top and bake for 15 minutes.

5. Sprinkle the hot casseroles with the cheese strips and bake for 5 minutes, or until the cheese is melted and the filling is bubbling.

SWEET AFTERTHOUGHT: *For a last-minute dessert, stir ¼ cup diced dried apricots and ¼ cup chopped almonds (toasted if desired) into instant vanilla or chocolate pudding. For an even richer version, make the pudding with half-and-half instead of milk.*

Pork-and-Sausage-Stuffed Golden Apples

SERVES 4

1 POUND LEAN GROUND PORK
½ POUND BULK PORK SAUSAGE
½ CUP MINCED ONION
4 LARGE GOLDEN DELICIOUS APPLES
¼ CUP FRESH LEMON JUICE
2 SLICES FIRM-TEXTURED WHITE
   BREAD, TORN INTO FINE CRUMBS

¼ CUP CHOPPED PARSLEY
1 TEASPOON SAGE
½ TEASPOON SALT
½ TEASPOON BLACK PEPPER
1 CUP APPLE CIDER

1. Preheat the oven to 350°.

2. In a large skillet, crumble in the pork and sausage, and cook over medium heat, stirring frequently, until no pink remains, 5 to 7 minutes. Transfer to a large bowl.

3. Add the onion to the drippings in the pan and cook, stirring frequently, until softened, about 3 minutes. Add the onion to the pork and sausage.

4. Core the apples, then cut a thin slice from the top of each. With a paring knife and teaspoon, carefully hollow out the apples, leaving a ¼-inch shell. Reserve the pulp for the stuffing mixture. Brush the inside of each shell with some of the lemon juice to prevent discoloration. Place the apples in an 8 x 8-inch baking dish.

5. Coarsely chop the reserved apple pulp. Add the chopped apple to the pork and sausage, and sprinkle the apple evenly with the remaining lemon juice. Add the bread crumbs, parsley, sage, salt, and pepper, and stir well to combine.

6. Fill each apple with some of the stuffing, mounding slightly. Place the remaining stuffing around the apples in the baking dish; spoon a little cider on top. Place the apples in the oven and bake for 40 minutes, or until they are tender, basting with the remaining cider every 10 minutes.

7. Transfer the apples to 4 plates and serve with the extra stuffing on the side.

HAM-AND-RICE-STUFFED PEPPERS

SERVES 4

4 VERY LARGE GREEN BELL PEPPERS

3 TABLESPOONS VEGETABLE OIL

1 CUP RICE

2 CUPS REDUCED-SODIUM CHICKEN
  BROTH

½ POUND PART-SKIM MOZZARELLA
  CHEESE

2 MEDIUM ONIONS, CHOPPED

4 GARLIC CLOVES, MINCED

4 MEDIUM MUSHROOMS, CHOPPED

ONE ¾-POUND HAM STEAK, CUT INTO
  ¼-INCH DICE

2 TABLESPOONS CHOPPED PARSLEY

1 TABLESPOON MINCED FRESH BASIL,
  OR 1 TEASPOON DRIED

¼ TEASPOON SALT

¼ TEASPOON BLACK PEPPER

PINCH OF CAYENNE PEPPER

1. Slice the tops off the bell peppers, chop, and set aside. Remove the ribs and seeds from the peppers. Steam the peppers in a vegetable steamer for 5 minutes. Remove the peppers from the steamer and drain upside down.

2. In a medium saucepan, warm 1 tablespoon of the oil over medium-high heat. Add the rice and sauté, stirring constantly, until well coated with the oil, about 5 minutes. Stir in the broth and bring to a boil. Reduce the heat to very low, cover, and simmer until the liquid is absorbed and the rice is tender, about 15 minutes.

3. Meanwhile, preheat the oven to 400°. Cut 4 thin slices from the mozzarella cheese and reserve; dice the remainder.

4. In a medium skillet, warm the remaining 2 tablespoons oil over medium heat. Add the onions and cook, stirring frequently, until translucent, about 3 minutes. Add the garlic and reserved chopped peppers, and cook, stirring frequently, for 4 minutes. Stir in the mushrooms and cook for 2 minutes. Transfer the onion mixture to a large bowl.

5. Add the diced ham and hot rice to the onion mixture, stirring to combine. Add the diced cheese, parsley, basil, salt, black pepper, and cayenne, and mix thoroughly.

6. Divide the stuffing mixture among the bell peppers. Transfer the peppers to a baking pan and bake for 20 minutes. Top each stuffed pepper with 1 slice of mozzarella and bake for 7 to 8 minutes, or until the cheese melts.

Beef-and-Onion Shepherd's Pie

SERVES 6

1 POUND SWEET POTATOES

1 TABLESPOON FLOUR

2 TABLESPOONS PAPRIKA

¾ TEASPOON GROUND GINGER

¾ TEASPOON SALT

½ TEASPOON BLACK PEPPER

⅛ TEASPOON ALLSPICE

2 TABLESPOONS OLIVE OIL

3 MEDIUM ONIONS, THINLY SLICED

½ POUND MUSHROOMS, THINLY SLICED

½ CUP BEEF BROTH

1 POUND ROAST BEEF (IN 2 THICK
   SLICES), CUT INTO ½-INCH CUBES

2 TABLESPOONS UNSALTED BUTTER

2 TEASPOONS BROWN SUGAR

1. Preheat the oven to 425°. Line a baking sheet with foil. With a sharp knife, cut 1 or 2 short slits in the sweet potatoes to act as steam vents. Bake the potatoes for 35 minutes, or until tender.

2. Meanwhile, in a small bowl, combine the flour, paprika, ¼ teaspoon of the ginger, the salt, pepper, and allspice, and stir to blend.

3. In a large nonstick skillet, warm 1 tablespoon of the oil over medium-high heat. Add the onions and cook, stirring frequently, until they begin to brown, about 5 minutes. Add the remaining 1 tablespoon oil and the mushrooms and cook until the mushrooms are softened, 2 to 3 minutes.

4. Stir in the seasoned flour and cook, stirring, until it is no longer visible, about 30 sec-

onds. Add the broth and bring the mixture to a boil, stirring until thickened, about 2 minutes. Add the roast beef to the skillet, stir well, and remove from the heat.

5. Remove the sweet potatoes from the oven and preheat the broiler. Halve the potatoes and scoop the flesh out into a medium bowl. Add the butter, brown sugar, and remaining ½ teaspoon ginger, and mash into the potatoes with a potato masher or fork.

6. Transfer the beef mixture to an ovenproof skillet or shallow baking dish. Spoon the mashed potatoes around the rim of the skillet on top of the beef mixture. Broil the pie for 3 to 4 minutes, or until the topping is lightly browned and the filling is heated through.

CHEESE MEAT LOAF WITH PARSLIED TOMATO SAUCE

SERVES 4

1½ POUNDS GROUND BEEF CHUCK

1 EGG

⅓ CUP FINE UNSEASONED DRY BREAD
CRUMBS

½ TEASPOON OREGANO

½ TEASPOON BASIL

¼ TEASPOON SALT

¼ TEASPOON BLACK PEPPER

6 SLICES OF PROVOLONE CHEESE

2 TABLESPOONS OLIVE OIL

½ CUP CHOPPED ONION

1 GARLIC CLOVE, MINCED

ONE 28-OUNCE CAN CRUSHED
TOMATOES

3 TABLESPOONS CHOPPED PARSLEY

1. Preheat the oven to 375°. Line a 13 x 9-inch baking dish with foil; set aside.

2. In a large bowl, combine the beef, egg, bread crumbs, oregano, basil, and ⅛ teaspoon each of the salt and pepper, and mix until well blended. Turn the mixture out onto a 15-inch-long sheet of foil and shape it into a 9-inch square.

3. Layer the cheese slices over the meat loaf, leaving a 1-inch border around the edges. Using the foil as an aid, roll the meat tightly, jelly-roll style, completely sealing the cheese inside the loaf. Transfer the meat loaf to the prepared baking dish, removing the foil used for rolling, and bake for 40 minutes.

4. Meanwhile, in a medium saucepan, warm the oil over medium-high heat. Add the onion and garlic, and cook, stirring frequently, until softened, about 3 minutes. Add the tomatoes and bring to a boil. Stir in the parsley, and remaining ⅛ teaspoon each salt and pepper. Reduce the heat to low and simmer until the sauce is slightly thickened, about 25 minutes. Set aside and keep warm until ready to serve.

5. Remove the meat loaf from the oven and set it aside to rest for 5 minutes. Cut the loaf into ½-inch-thick slices and serve topped with the parslied tomato sauce.

İtalian Meat Loaf with Tomato Sauce

SERVES 4

1½ POUNDS PORK TENDERLOIN,
  GROUND OR VERY FINELY CHOPPED
3 GARLIC CLOVES, MINCED
¼ CUP FRESH BREAD CRUMBS
¼ CUP MINCED PLUS ⅓ CUP COARSELY
  CHOPPED FRESH BASIL
2 TABLESPOONS DRY WHITE WINE
2 TABLESPOONS PLUS 2 TEASPOONS
  MINCED SUN-DRIED TOMATOES

1 TABLESPOON TOMATO PASTE
¼ TEASPOON BLACK PEPPER
1 TABLESPOON OLIVE OIL
1 LARGE ONION, FINELY CHOPPED
ONE 28-OUNCE CAN NO-SALT-ADDED
  WHOLE TOMATOES
1 BAY LEAF
1 TABLESPOON UNSALTED BUTTER
½ POUND MUSHROOMS, CHOPPED

1. Preheat the oven to 350°. Line a 9 x 5-inch loaf pan with wax paper.

2. In a large bowl, combine the pork, one-third of the garlic, the bread crumbs, minced basil, wine, 2 tablespoons of the sun-dried tomatoes, the tomato paste, and ⅛ teaspoon of the black pepper, and mix them together well. Press the meat loaf mixture into the prepared pan and bake for 1 hour.

3. Meanwhile, in a large skillet, warm the oil over medium heat. Add the onion and remaining garlic, and cook, stirring frequently, until they are translucent, about 5 minutes. Add the canned tomatoes, breaking them up with the back of a spoon. Stir in the bay leaf,

the 2 teaspoons minced sun-dried tomatoes, and the remaining ⅛ teaspoon black pepper, and cook, stirring occasionally, until the sauce is slightly thickened, about 20 minutes.

4. Meanwhile, in a medium nonstick skillet, warm the butter over medium-high heat until melted. Add the mushrooms and cook, stirring frequently, until softened, about 3 minutes. Add the mushrooms and the ⅓ cup chopped basil to the sauce and stir well to combine.

5. Serve the meat loaf cut into thick slices with the sauce spooned around it.

Cajun Meat Loaf

SERVES 6

1 TABLESPOON OLIVE OIL

1 MEDIUM ONION, COARSELY CHOPPED

4 GARLIC CLOVES, MINCED

3 TABLESPOONS CHILI POWDER

1 TEASPOON PAPRIKA

¾ TEASPOON SALT

PINCH OF CAYENNE PEPPER

1 CUP TOMATO JUICE

1 POUND GROUND BEEF

1 POUND GROUND PORK

2 SLICES WHOLE WHEAT OR WHITE
  BREAD, TORN INTO SMALL PIECES

2 EGGS, LIGHTLY BEATEN

2 TABLESPOONS WORCESTERSHIRE
  SAUCE

½ TEASPOON SUGAR

¼ TEASPOON HOT PEPPER SAUCE

1. Preheat the oven to 350°.

2. In a large skillet, warm the oil over high heat. Add the onion, garlic, chili powder, paprika, salt, and cayenne. Cover, reduce the heat to low, and cook, stirring occasionally, until the onion is softened but not browned, about 10 minutes. Remove the skillet from the heat, stir in the tomato juice, and set the mixture aside to cool slightly.

3. In a large bowl, combine the beef and pork. Add the bread, eggs, Worcestershire sauce, sugar, hot pepper sauce, and onion mixture and mix lightly but thoroughly. Place the mixture in a 9 x 5-inch loaf pan.

4. Bake the meat loaf for 55 minutes, or until a meat thermometer inserted in the center registers 160°. Let stand for 5 to 10 minutes before slicing.

Variation: *For a lighter meat loaf, use ground turkey in place of either the ground beef or the ground pork. If you use a combination of turkey and pork—which will be more delicately flavored than a meat loaf made with beef—reduce the chili powder to 2 tablespoons and use tomato-vegetable juice instead of plain tomato juice.*

BROILED VEAL CHOPS
WITH WINTER VEGETABLE SAUTÉ

SERVES 4

1 TABLESPOON PLUS 1 TEASPOON OLIVE
  OIL
1 TABLESPOON PLUS 1 TEASPOON
  PAPRIKA
¾ TEASPOON BLACK PEPPER
4 VEAL LOIN CHOPS (½ INCH THICK,
  ABOUT 1½ POUNDS TOTAL)
1 LARGE ONION, COARSELY CHOPPED
3 GARLIC CLOVES, MINCED

2 LARGE CARROTS, COARSELY CHOPPED
½ POUND CABBAGE, SHREDDED
1 CELERY RIB, COARSELY CHOPPED
¼ CUP CHICKEN BROTH
1 TEASPOON CUMIN SEED OR GROUND
  CUMIN
¼ TEASPOON SALT
PINCH OF SUGAR

1. Preheat the broiler. Line a broiler pan with foil.

2. In a small bowl, combine 2 teaspoons of the olive oil, 2 teaspoons of the paprika, and ½ teaspoon of the pepper. Brush the veal chops with the paprika oil and place them on the prepared broiler pan. Set aside.

3. In a large nonstick skillet, warm the remaining 2 teaspoons oil over medium-high heat until hot but not smoking. Add the onion and garlic, and stir-fry until the onion begins to brown, about 5 minutes.

4. Add the carrots, cabbage, celery, broth, cumin, salt, sugar, and the remaining 2 teaspoons paprika and ¼ teaspoon pepper. Cook, stirring, until the vegetables are just limp, 5 to 8 minutes.

5. Meanwhile, broil the veal chops 4 inches from the heat for 4 minutes. Turn and broil until cooked through, about 4 minutes.

6. Serve the chops with the vegetable sauté on the side.

LONDON BROIL
WITH CHILI SEASONINGS

SERVES 6

♦ EXTRA-QUICK

3 TABLESPOONS OLIVE OIL

1 TABLESPOON WORCESTERSHIRE
SAUCE

3 GARLIC CLOVES, MINCED

¼ CUP CHOPPED PARSLEY

3 TABLESPOONS CHILI POWDER

2 TEASPOONS CUMIN

2 TEASPOONS PAPRIKA

½ TEASPOON SALT

¼ TEASPOON BLACK PEPPER

PINCH OF CAYENNE PEPPER

1½ POUNDS LONDON BROIL

1. Preheat the broiler. Line a broiler pan with foil.

2. In a small bowl, combine the oil, Worcestershire sauce, garlic, parsley, chili powder, cumin, paprika, salt, black pepper, and cayenne.

3. Place the steak on the broiler pan and brush with half of the marinade. Broil the steak 4 inches from the heat for 7 minutes.

4. Turn the steak over, brush the other side with the remaining marinade, and broil 4 inches from the heat until well browned: about 7 minutes for medium-rare, 9 minutes for medium, 11 minutes for well-done. Let the steak stand for 5 minutes before slicing.

5. To serve, cut the steak into thin slices across the grain and on the diagonal.

KITCHEN NOTE: *A number of different cuts, including flank steak and top round, are marketed as London broil. These cuts are generally pretty lean, so an oil-based marinade, as here, is often used to keep the meat moist and juicy. Another trick for "tenderizing" these steaks is to cook them on the rare side and then carve them into thin diagonal slices across the grain.*

London Broil Teriyaki

SERVES 6

1 CUP REDUCED-SODIUM SOY SAUCE

¼ CUP VEGETABLE OIL

¼ CUP APRICOT JAM

1 TABLESPOON PLUS 1 TEASPOON
CORNSTARCH

¼ TEASPOON BLACK PEPPER

3 GARLIC CLOVES, PEELED

2 POUNDS TOP ROUND (1¼ INCHES
THICK)

12 MUSHROOM CAPS

24 CHERRY TOMATOES

1. Preheat the broiler or prepare the grill. If broiling, line a baking sheet with foil.

2. In a small saucepan, combine the soy sauce, oil, apricot jam, cornstarch, pepper, and whole garlic cloves. Stir to blend, then bring to a boil over medium heat, stirring. Remove from the heat.

3. Brush the steak with the teriyaki sauce. (If broiling, place the steak on the baking sheet before brushing it with the sauce.) Broil or grill the steak 4 inches from the heat, turning once and brushing the second side with teriyaki sauce: 5 to 7 minutes per side for rare, 8 to 10 minutes per side for medium-rare, 11 to 13 minutes per side for well-done.

4. Meanwhile, dividing the mushroom caps and tomatoes evenly, thread them onto skewers. About 4 minutes before the steak is done, brush the skewered vegetables with some teriyaki sauce and place them on the grill or under the broiler for 2 minutes. Turn them over, brush with more teriyaki sauce and cook for 2 minutes longer.

5. Cut the steak into thin slices across the grain and on the diagonal. Serve with the skewered vegetables. Remove and discard the garlic from the remaining teriyaki sauce, and bring it to a boil before serving it alongside the steak.

Sirloin Steak with Dijon and Herbed Potatoes

SERVES 4

1 POUND SMALL UNPEELED RED
   POTATOES, HALVED
2 TABLESPOONS UNSALTED BUTTER,
   MELTED
¼ CUP CHOPPED PARSLEY
4 GARLIC CLOVES, MINCED
1½ TEASPOONS TARRAGON
¾ TEASPOON SALT

¼ TEASPOON GROUND BLACK PEPPER
2 TABLESPOONS RED WINE VINEGAR
3 TABLESPOONS DIJON MUSTARD
1 TEASPOON DRY MUSTARD
½ TEASPOON CRACKED BLACK PEPPER
2 MEDIUM SIRLOIN STEAKS (ABOUT 1½
   POUNDS TOTAL)

1. Preheat the broiler. Line a broiler pan with foil.

2. Add the potatoes to a saucepan of boiling water. Let the water return to a boil, then reduce the heat to medium-low, cover, and cook for 10 minutes. Drain and toss with the melted butter, 2 tablespoons of the parsley, half of the garlic, ½ teaspoon of the tarragon, ¼ of the teaspoon salt, and the ground black pepper.

3. Meanwhile, in a small bowl, combine the vinegar, Dijon mustard, dry mustard, cracked pepper, and the remaining garlic, 1 teaspoon tarragon, and ½ teaspoon salt.

4. Place the steaks on the broiler pan and brush with half the mustard mixture. Arrange the potatoes around the steaks and broil 4 inches from the heat for 7 minutes.

5. Turn the steaks and potatoes over. Brush the steaks with the remaining mustard mixture. Broil for 7 minutes for rare, 9 minutes for medium-rare, 11 minutes for medium. Let the steaks rest 5 minutes before slicing across the grain. Serve with the potatoes and some of the pan juices. Garnish with the remaining parsley.

LONDON BROIL WITH CARAMELIZED ONIONS

SERVES 6

◆ EXTRA-QUICK

1 TABLESPOON OLIVE OIL

2 TABLESPOONS UNSALTED BUTTER

4 MEDIUM ONIONS, SLICED

3 GARLIC CLOVES, MINCED

2 TEASPOONS SUGAR

1½ POUNDS LONDON BROIL

¼ CUP BEEF BROTH

2 TABLESPOONS DRY SHERRY

¼ TEASPOON SALT

¼ TEASPOON BLACK PEPPER

1. Preheat the broiler. Line a broiler pan with foil.

2. In a medium skillet, warm the oil with the butter over medium-high heat until the butter is melted. Add the onions and garlic, and cook, stirring, until the onion begins to brown, about 5 minutes. Add the sugar to the onions and cook 5 minutes longer.

3. Meanwhile, broil the steak 4 inches from the heat for 8 minutes on one side. Turn the steak over and broil for 7 minutes for rare, 10 minutes for medium-rare, 11 to 12 minutes for medium.

4. Add the broth and sherry to the skillet and bring the liquid to a boil over medium-high heat. Reduce the heat to low and cook, uncovered, until ready to slice the steak, about 15 minutes, stirring occasionally. Season with the salt and pepper.

5. Let the steak rest for about 5 minutes, then slice it across the grain and on the diagonal. Serve the steak with the caramelized onions on the side.

STEAK WITH LEMON-PEPPER CRUST

SERVES 4

◆ EXTRA-QUICK

2 LEMONS
TWO T-BONE STEAKS (ABOUT 2½
   POUNDS TOTAL)
4 SCALLIONS, COARSELY CHOPPED

4 GARLIC CLOVES, MINCED
2 TABLESPOONS CRACKED BLACK
   PEPPER

1. Preheat the broiler or prepare the grill. If broiling, line a broiler pan with foil.

2. Grate the zest from the lemons, then juice them.

3. Place the steaks in a shallow pan and pour the lemon juice over them. Let stand while you prepare the remaining ingredients and while the broiler or grill is preheating. Turn the steaks over after about 5 minutes.

4. In a small bowl, combine the lemon zest, scallions, garlic, and cracked pepper.

5. Remove the steaks from the lemon juice. (If broiling, place the steaks on the prepared broiler pan.) Press half of the lemon-pepper mixture onto the top sides of the steaks. Grill or broil the steaks 4 inches from the heat for 7 minutes.

6. Turn the steaks over and press the remaining lemon-pepper mixture onto them. Grill or broil 4 inches from the heat for 7 minutes for rare, 9 minutes for medium-rare, 11 minutes for medium to well-done.

7. Let the steaks stand for 5 minutes before slicing.

SUBSTITUTION: *You can find coarsely cracked black pepper in a jar in your supermarket's spice section, but for even fresher flavor, buy whole peppercorns and crush them yourself. Place the peppercorns on a cutting board, lay the flat side of a heavy knife or cleaver over them, and give it a sharp rap with your fist.*

HERB-MARINATED STEAK

SERVES 4

⅓ CUP RED WINE VINEGAR

⅓ CUP REDUCED-SODIUM SOY SAUCE

⅓ CUP WORCESTERSHIRE SAUCE

¼ CUP (PACKED) LIGHT BROWN SUGAR

1 TEASPOON OREGANO

½ TEASPOON BASIL

1½ POUNDS BONELESS SIRLOIN STEAK
   (1 INCH THICK)

1. Combine the vinegar, soy sauce, Worcestershire sauce, brown sugar, oregano, and basil in a 13 x 9 x 2-inch glass or ceramic dish. Add the steak and set aside to marinate for about 30 minutes at room temperature.

2. Preheat the broiler. Broil the steak for 8 minutes. Turn the steak over, brush with the marinade, and broil 7 minutes for rare, 8 minutes for medium, 10 minutes for well-done.

3. Transfer the steak to a serving platter and let rest for 5 minutes before slicing.

VARIATION: *The combination of oregano and basil gives the steak a somewhat Italian flavor; for a change, substitute 1½ teaspoons of dried rosemary for the two herbs. Or use 1 tablespoon of crushed fresh rosemary instead of dried. Be sure to crush dried rosemary (and chop fresh rosemary) to release its flavor and fragrance.*

STEAK WITH HORSERADISH-MUSHROOM CREAM

SERVES 4

◆ EXTRA-QUICK

2 BONELESS RIB-EYE OR CLUB STEAKS
   (ABOUT 1½ POUNDS TOTAL)
1 TABLESPOON OLIVE OIL
2 TABLESPOONS UNSALTED BUTTER
4 SCALLIONS, COARSELY CHOPPED
2 GARLIC CLOVES, MINCED
½ POUND MUSHROOMS, SLICED

½ CUP BEEF BROTH
1 TABLESPOON CORNSTARCH
2 TABLESPOONS HORSERADISH
1 TEASPOON THYME
¼ TEASPOON BLACK PEPPER
¼ CUP SOUR CREAM

1. Preheat the broiler. Line a broiler pan with foil.

2. Place the steaks on the prepared broiler pan and broil 4 inches from the heat for 7 minutes. Turn the steaks over and broil for 7 minutes for rare, 9 minutes for medium-rare, 11 minutes for medium to well-done. Let the steaks rest for 5 minutes before slicing them.

3. Meanwhile, in a medium skillet, warm the oil with the butter over medium-high heat until the butter is melted. Add the scallions and garlic, and cook until the scallions are softened, about 1 minute. Add the mush-rooms and cook, stirring, until they start to wilt, about 3 minutes.

4. In a small bowl, combine the beef broth and cornstarch. Stir this mixture, the horse-radish, thyme, and pepper into the skillet. Bring the mixture to a boil over medium heat and cook, stirring, until slightly thickened, 1 to 2 minutes. Stir in the sour cream and re-move the horseradish-mushroom cream from the heat.

5. Serve slices of the steak topped with some of the horseradish-mushroom cream.

GRILLED STEAKS WITH RED WINE-MUSHROOM SAUCE

SERVES 4

1 CUP DRY RED WINE

2 TABLESPOONS REDUCED-SODIUM SOY SAUCE

1 TABLESPOON RED WINE VINEGAR

1 TEASPOON THYME

¼ TEASPOON BLACK PEPPER

4 GARLIC CLOVES, MINCED

4 SMALL NEW YORK SIRLOIN STEAKS (ABOUT 1¾ POUNDS TOTAL)

2 TABLESPOONS UNSALTED BUTTER

4 SCALLIONS, COARSELY CHOPPED

¾ POUND MUSHROOMS, THINLY SLICED

2 TABLESPOONS FLOUR

1. In a shallow dish large enough to hold the steaks in a single layer, combine the wine, soy sauce, vinegar, thyme, pepper, and half of the garlic. Place the steaks in the marinade and turn them over to thoroughly coat. Set them aside to marinate while you prepare the remaining ingredients.

2. Preheat the broiler or prepare the grill. If broiling, line a broiler pan with foil.

3. In a medium skillet, melt the butter over medium-high heat. Add the remaining garlic, the scallions, and mushrooms, and sauté until the scallions are limp and the mushrooms are beginning to release their liquid, 2 to 3 minutes. Stir in the flour and cook, stirring, until it is no longer visible, about 30 seconds.

4. Remove the steaks from the marinade, reserving the marinade. Stir the reserved marinade into the skillet and cook, stirring, until the mixture has come to a boil and thickened slightly, 1 to 2 minutes. Reduce the heat to low and simmer while you cook the steaks.

5. Grill or broil the steaks 4 inches from the heat: 7 minutes per side for rare, 8 minutes per side for medium-rare, 9 minutes per side for well-done. Let the steaks rest for 5 minutes before serving.

6. Serve the steaks topped with the red wine-mushroom sauce.

Skirt Steak with Black Bean Chili Sauce

SERVES 4

◆ EXTRA-QUICK

1 TABLESPOON UNSALTED BUTTER

1 MEDIUM ONION, COARSELY CHOPPED

3 GARLIC CLOVES, MINCED

1 CUP CANNED NO-SALT-ADDED
    STEWED TOMATOES, WITH JUICE

1 TABLESPOON CORNSTARCH

ONE 15-OUNCE CAN BLACK BEANS,
    RINSED AND DRAINED

3 TABLESPOONS FRESH LIME JUICE

2 TABLESPOONS CHILI POWDER

2 TEASPOONS PAPRIKA

½ TEASPOON SALT

⅛ TEASPOON CAYENNE PEPPER

1 TABLESPOON OLIVE OIL

1 POUND SKIRT STEAK

1. Preheat the broiler. Line a broiler pan with foil.

2. In a medium skillet, warm the butter over medium-high heat until melted. Add the onion and garlic, and cook, stirring, until the onion is translucent, about 5 minutes.

3. Meanwhile, drain the stewed tomatoes in a strainer set over a small bowl. Stir the cornstarch into the tomato liquid.

4. Add the stewed tomatoes, the cornstarch-tomato mixture, black beans, 1½ tablespoons of the lime juice, 1 tablespoon of the chili powder, 1 teaspoon of the paprika, the salt, and cayenne to the skillet. Bring to a boil over medium-high heat and cook, stirring, until

slightly thickened, 1 to 2 minutes. Keep warm while you broil the steak.

5. In a small bowl, combine the oil, the remaining 1½ tablespoons lime juice, 1 tablespoon chili powder, and 1 teaspoon paprika. Place the steak on the broiler pan. Brush with half of the basting mixture and broil 4 inches from the heat for 3 minutes. Turn the steak over, brush with the remaining basting mixture, and broil for 3 minutes for medium-rare.

6. Let the steak rest for 5 minutes before slicing across the grain on the diagonal. Top with the chili sauce.

GRILLED STEAKS
WITH MUSTARD-YOGURT SAUCE

SERVES 4

FOUR 5-OUNCE SIRLOIN STEAKS
2 TABLESPOONS GRAINY MUSTARD
2 GARLIC CLOVES, MINCED

⅔ CUP PLAIN LOW-FAT YOGURT
½ TEASPOON BLACK PEPPER

1. Starting at the untrimmed side of each steak, cut a pocket almost through to the opposite side. Coat the insides of the pockets with half of the grainy mustard, then rub the steaks all over with half of the garlic. Place the steaks in a dish and set them aside to marinate for 30 minutes at room temperature.

2. Meanwhile, in a bowl, combine the yogurt, pepper, and the remaining mustard and garlic.

3. Preheat the broiler or prepare the grill. Brush the grill or broiler rack with oil and cook the steaks 4 inches from the heat for 5 to 7 minutes on each side. Serve the steaks with the sauce.

SWEET AFTERTHOUGHT: *While you have the fire going, you might as well grill your dessert. Try this variation on an all-American backyard treat: Start with four firm-ripe bananas. Cut a slit the length of each banana (without going all the way to the ends or through to the other side). Stuff the slits with coarsely chopped butterscotch chips and miniature marshmallows. Wrap each banana in foil and place on the grill or in the coals until the filling has melted.*

Sirloin and Leek Skewers with Ginger Chutney

SERVES 4

One 2-inch piece fresh ginger, cut into large chunks

½ small onion, cut into large chunks

1 tart apple, peeled and quartered

½ cup golden raisins

½ cup fresh lime juice

1 tablespoon honey

¼ teaspoon grainy mustard

1 teaspoon cayenne pepper

½ teaspoon ground white pepper

½ teaspoon allspice

½ teaspoon cumin

½ teaspoon turmeric

¼ teaspoon salt

1¼ pounds boneless sirloin steak, cut into long, thin strips

3 leeks, white parts only, cut lengthwise into ½-inch-wide strips

1. In a food processor or blender, chop the ginger, onion, and apple. Add the raisins, lime juice, honey, and mustard, and pulse on and off to form a coarse paste. Transfer the chutney to a bowl and refrigerate until serving time.

2. Preheat the broiler or prepare the grill.

3. In a small bowl, combine the cayenne, white pepper, allspice, cumin, turmeric, and salt. Spread the strips of beef on a baking sheet or tray. With your fingers, rub the spice mixture into the beef. Set the beef aside.

4. Blanch the leeks in a large saucepan of boiling water for 2 minutes. Drain them and rinse under cold running water.

5. Lay a strip of leek on top of each piece of meat. Divide the meat and leeks among 12 skewers, threading the skewer through both leek and meat at frequent intervals.

6. Grill or broil the skewers for 1 minute on each side for medium-rare meat, and serve them with the ginger chutney.

Barbecued Beef Kebabs

SERVES 4

16 LARGE SHALLOTS

¼ CUP OLIVE OIL

¼ CUP ORIENTAL (DARK) SESAME OIL

¼ CUP REDUCED-SODIUM SOY SAUCE

2 TABLESPOONS CHOPPED FRESH
ROSEMARY, OR 2 TEASPOONS DRIED

1 TABLESPOON GRATED ORANGE ZEST

1 TEASPOON MINCED GARLIC

½ TEASPOON BLACK PEPPER

1½ POUNDS BEEF TENDERLOIN, CUT
INTO 1¼-INCH CUBES

1 TABLESPOON PLUS 1 TEASPOON
SESAME SEEDS

1. Blanch the unpeeled shallots (or onions) in a saucepan of boiling water for 1 minute. Drain and refresh under cold running water.

2. In a baking dish, combine the olive oil, sesame oil, soy sauce, rosemary, orange zest, garlic, and pepper. Add the beef and shallots, and gently toss until coated. Cover with plastic wrap and marinate for at least 20 minutes, stirring and turning occasionally.

3. Meanwhile, prepare the grill.

4. Reserving the marinade, thread the shallots and beef onto skewers. Grill the kebabs 5 to 6 inches from the heat for 2 to 3 minutes per side, or until the beef is seared and brown.

5. Baste the kebabs with the reserved marinade and grill, turning frequently, for 8 to 10 minutes for rare, 10 to 12 minutes for medium-rare, and 12 to 16 minutes for well-done.

6. Sprinkle the kebabs with the sesame seeds and serve.

SUBSTITUTION: *If you can't get shallots—or if there are no large ones available—use small white onions instead. Try to find onions no bigger than 1 inch in diameter. The instructions for blanching are the same as for the shallots.*

Tomato-Grilled Pork Chops

SERVES 4

ONE 6-OUNCE CAN TOMATO-
    VEGETABLE JUICE
3 GARLIC CLOVES, MINCED
¼ CUP RED WINE VINEGAR OR CIDER
    VINEGAR
3 TABLESPOONS OLIVE OIL
1½ TEASPOONS BASIL
1½ TEASPOONS OREGANO
½ TEASPOON BLACK PEPPER
4 LOIN PORK CHOPS (¾ INCH THICK,
    ABOUT 1¾ POUNDS TOTAL)

1 TEASPOON DIJON MUSTARD
¼ TEASPOON SALT
1 CUP CANNED WHITE BEANS, RINSED
    AND DRAINED
1 SMALL RED ONION, CUT INTO THIN
    RINGS
1 TABLESPOON CORNSTARCH
2 CUPS (PACKED) FRESH SPINACH
    LEAVES, TORN INTO BITE-SIZE PIECES
1 MEDIUM TOMATO, CUT INTO THIN
    WEDGES

1. In a shallow baking dish large enough to hold the chops in one layer, combine the tomato-vegetable juice, garlic, 2 tablespoons of the vinegar, 1 tablespoon of the oil, 1 teaspoon each of the basil and oregano, and ¼ teaspoon of the pepper. Add the chops and turn to coat all over. Set aside to marinate while you prepare the grill.

2. Preheat the broiler or prepare the grill.

3. In a salad bowl, combine the mustard with the salt and the remaining 2 tablespoons vinegar, 2 tablespoons oil, ½ teaspoon each basil and oregano, and ¼ teaspoon pepper. Add the beans and onion and toss to coat.

4. Reserving the marinade, grill or broil the chops 4 inches from the heat until browned all over and cooked through, 6 to 8 minutes per side.

5. Meanwhile, pour the marinade into a small saucepan and combine it with the cornstarch. Bring the mixture to a boil over medium-high heat, stirring constantly until slightly thickened, 2 to 3 minutes.

6. Add the spinach and tomato to the bowl with the beans and onion, and toss to coat with the dressing.

7. Serve the chops with the salad and pass the thickened marinade on the side.

HONEY-APRICOT SPARERIBS

SERVES 4

¼ CUP APRICOT JAM

3 TABLESPOONS REDUCED-SODIUM SOY
SAUCE

3 TABLESPOONS HONEY

1 TEASPOON CHILI POWDER

2 POUNDS SPARERIBS

1 TABLESPOON VEGETABLE OIL

4 QUARTER-SIZE SLICES FRESH GINGER,
MINCED

3 GARLIC CLOVES, MINCED

1 MEDIUM ONION, COARSELY CHOPPED

⅓ CUP CHICKEN BROTH

¼ CUP ORANGE JUICE

3 TABLESPOONS KETCHUP

2 TEASPOONS GRATED ORANGE ZEST

1. Preheat the broiler. Line a broiler pan with foil.

2. In a small bowl, combine 2 tablespoons of the apricot jam, 2 tablespoons of the soy sauce, 2 tablespoons of the honey, and the chili powder.

3. Place the spareribs on the broiler pan and brush with half of the honey-apricot basting mixture. Broil 4 inches from the heat until golden brown, 7 to 10 minutes. Turn the spareribs over and brush them with the remaining basting mixture. Broil until golden brown (with dark patches), 7 to 10 minutes.

4. Meanwhile, in a large skillet, warm the oil over medium-high heat until hot but not smoking. Add the ginger, garlic, and onion, and stir-fry until the onion begins to brown, about 5 minutes.

5. Add the broth, orange juice, ketchup, orange zest, and the remaining 2 tablespoons apricot jam, 1 tablespoon soy sauce, and 1 tablespoon honey to the skillet. Bring the mixture to a boil, then reduce the heat to low, cover, and simmer until the spareribs are finished cooking.

6. Cut the spareribs into sections. Increase the heat under the sauce to medium-high and add the ribs (and any pan juices from the broiler pan). Let the mixture return to a boil, then reduce the heat to medium-low, cover, and simmer until the ribs are tender and cooked through, 20 to 25 minutes.

7. Serve the ribs with the sauce on the side.

Indonesian-Style Grilled Pork

SERVES 4

¼ CUP REDUCED-SODIUM SOY SAUCE

1 TABLESPOON RICE WINE VINEGAR OR
WHITE WINE VINEGAR

1 TABLESPOON VEGETABLE OIL

2 TABLESPOONS SUGAR

2 TEASPOONS MINCED GARLIC

1 TEASPOON GROUND CORIANDER

1 TEASPOON GROUND GINGER

1 TEASPOON SALT

2 POUNDS BONELESS BLADE BOSTON
PORK ROAST, CUT INTO 1-INCH
CUBES

1. In a large bowl, blend the soy sauce, vinegar, oil, sugar, garlic, coriander, ginger, and salt. Add the pork, stir until evenly coated, and set aside to marinate for 15 minutes.

2. Preheat the broiler or prepare the grill. If broiling, line a broiler pan with foil.

3. Reserving the marinade, divide the pork evenly among 8 skewers.

4. Broil or grill the meat 6 to 7 inches from the heat, turning the skewers occasionally and basting, for about 20 minutes, or until the meat is a rich brown.

KITCHEN NOTE: *Rice wine vinegar, used in many Asian cuisines, is milder than distilled white vinegar or white wine vinegar. In addition to its use in marinades, this delicate vinegar makes delicious salad dressings. Look for rice wine vinegar in the ethnic foods section of your supermarket, or at an Asian food store.*

BROILED PORK CHOPS WITH NECTARINE CHUTNEY

SERVES 4

♦ EXTRA-QUICK

1 POUND NECTARINES, COARSELY
   CHOPPED
1 SMALL ONION, COARSELY CHOPPED
1 TABLESPOON MINCED FRESH GINGER
1½ TEASPOONS GRATED LEMON ZEST
2 TABLESPOONS FRESH LEMON JUICE
1 TABLESPOON ORANGE JUICE
   CONCENTRATE

1 TABLESPOON CIDER VINEGAR
2 TABLESPOONS BROWN SUGAR
1 TABLESPOON CINNAMON
1 TABLESPOON OLIVE OIL
¼ TEASPOON BLACK PEPPER
4 CENTER-CUT LOIN PORK CHOPS
   (¼ INCH THICK, ABOUT 1 POUND
   TOTAL)

1. In a medium saucepan, combine the nectarines, onion, 1½ teaspoons of the ginger, the lemon zest, 1 tablespoon of the lemon juice, the orange juice concentrate, vinegar, brown sugar, and 1½ teaspoons of the cinnamon. Bring to a boil over medium-high heat. Reduce the heat to low, cover, and simmer while you broil the pork chops.

2. Preheat the broiler. Line a broiler pan with foil.

3. In a small bowl, combine the olive oil, pepper, and the remaining 1 tablespoon lemon juice, 1½ teaspoons ginger, and 1½ teaspoons cinnamon.

4. Place the pork chops on the prepared broiler pan. Brush them with half the olive oil mixture and broil 4 inches from the heat for 4 minutes.

5. Turn the pork chops over, brush them with the remaining olive oil mixture, and broil for 4 minutes, or until cooked through.

6. Serve the chops with the nectarine chutney on the side.

Honey-Glazed Pork Tenderloin

SERVES 6

◇ LOW-FAT

3 SCALLIONS, MINCED

1 QUARTER-SIZE SLICE FRESH GINGER, MINCED

2 GARLIC CLOVES, MINCED

¼ CUP FROZEN APPLE JUICE CONCENTRATE

2 TABLESPOONS REDUCED-SODIUM SOY SAUCE

2 TABLESPOONS HONEY

¼ TEASPOON BLACK PEPPER

1½ POUNDS LEAN CENTER-CUT PORK TENDERLOIN

1. Preheat the broiler or prepare the grill. If broiling, line a broiler pan with foil.

2. In a small bowl, combine the scallions, ginger, garlic, apple juice concentrate, soy sauce, honey, and pepper.

3. Brush the pork with some of the glaze. (If broiling, place the tenderloin on the broiler pan before brushing with the glaze.) Broil or grill the pork 4 inches from the heat until golden, 30 to 40 minutes. While it is cooking, turn it every 7 minutes or so and brush with more glaze.

4. To serve, cut the tenderloin into thin slices.

KITCHEN NOTE: *Fresh ginger is a mainstay of cooks who want to prepare low-fat dishes that are high in flavor. Buy a firm, glossy piece of ginger root with a paper-thin skin. If you don't use ginger often, but wish to keep it on hand, wrap the root tightly in plastic wrap and store it in the freezer. There's no need to thaw the ginger before slicing or grating it; if the skin is thin, you needn't peel it.*

PORK STRIPS WITH DIPPING SAUCE

SERVES 4

◆ EXTRA-QUICK

1 POUND BONELESS PORK LOIN

3 TABLESPOONS REDUCED-SODIUM SOY
   SAUCE

1 TABLESPOON ORIENTAL (DARK)
   SESAME OIL

2 TEASPOONS HONEY

3 GARLIC CLOVES, MINCED

6 QUARTER-SIZE SLICES FRESH GINGER,
   MINCED

1 TEASPOON GROUND CORIANDER

¼ CUP CREAMY PEANUT BUTTER

ABOUT 3 TABLESPOONS CHICKEN
   BROTH

1 TABLESPOON RICE WINE VINEGAR OR
   DISTILLED WHITE VINEGAR

3 TABLESPOONS CHOPPED CILANTRO

1. Preheat the broiler. Line a broiler pan with foil.

2. Cut the pork loin in half crosswise, then cut each half lengthwise into thin strips. Thread the pork strips onto skewers and place the skewers on the broiler pan.

3. In a small bowl, combine the soy sauce, 2 teaspoons of the sesame oil, the honey, garlic, half of the ginger, and the ground coriander.

4. Brush the pork with the basting mixture and broil 4 inches from the heat for 5 minutes. Turn the pork over and broil for 4 minutes, or until the pork is cooked through.

5. Meanwhile, in a small bowl, blend the peanut butter, 3 tablespoons of the chicken broth, the vinegar, cilantro, and the remaining 1 teaspoon sesame oil and remaining ginger. When the pork is done, stir any pan juices into the peanut dipping sauce. (You should have about 3 tablespoons of pan juices; if not, use additional chicken broth to make up the difference.)

6. Serve the pork with the dipping sauce on the side.

SAUSAGE AND POTATO KEBABS WITH MUSTARD GLAZE

SERVES 4

8 SMALL UNPEELED RED POTATOES,
   HALVED
3 TABLESPOONS OLIVE OIL
1 TABLESPOON DIJON MUSTARD
¼ TEASPOON BLACK PEPPER

2 MEDIUM ZUCCHINI, CUT INTO
   16 PIECES
1 POUND KIELBASA OR OTHER FULLY
   COOKED GARLIC SAUSAGE, CUT INTO
   16 PIECES

1. Preheat the broiler or prepare the grill. If broiling, line a baking sheet with foil.

2. Meanwhile, cook the potatoes in a saucepan of boiling water until just barely tender when pierced with a knife, 10 to 12 minutes. Drain well.

3. In a small bowl, combine the oil, mustard, and pepper.

4. Dividing the ingredients evenly, thread the potatoes, zucchini, and kielbasa alternately on skewers. Brush the kebabs lightly with the mustard glaze. (If broiling, place the kebabs on the foil-lined baking sheet before brushing them with the glaze.)

5. Broil or grill the kebabs 4 inches from the heat, turning once, until the kielbasa is lightly browned, 6 to 8 minutes.

Variation: *For a change of color scheme, use Yukon Gold or Yellow Finn potatoes instead of red potatoes in this recipe. These varieties have tan skin and appetizingly golden flesh. Try these yellow-fleshed potatoes baked or boiled, too—their buttery color might help you forego high-fat toppings.*

LAMB CHOPS
WITH CUCUMBER-MINT SALSA

SERVES 4

◆ EXTRA-QUICK

2 TABLESPOONS OLIVE OIL

4 GARLIC CLOVES, MINCED

⅓ CUP (PACKED) FRESH MINT LEAVES,
    MINCED, OR 1 TABLESPOON DRIED

¾ TEASPOON SALT

½ TEASPOON BLACK PEPPER

8 SMALL LOIN LAMB CHOPS (ABOUT
    2¼ POUNDS TOTAL)

1 MEDIUM CUCUMBER, PEELED AND
    COARSELY CHOPPED

2 TABLESPOONS CIDER VINEGAR

2 TEASPOONS SUGAR

PINCH OF CAYENNE PEPPER

1. Preheat the broiler or prepare the grill. If broiling, line a broiler pan with foil.

2. In a small bowl, combine the oil, garlic, half of the mint, ½ teaspoon of the salt, and the pepper.

3. Brush the chops with half of the mint oil. (If broiling, place the chops on the broiler pan first.) Broil or grill the chops 4 inches from the heat for 8 minutes.

4. Turn the chops over, brush with the remaining mint oil, and broil or grill 4 inches from the heat for 8 minutes for medium-rare, 10 minutes for medium, 12 minutes for well-done.

5. Meanwhile, in a medium bowl, combine the cucumber, vinegar, sugar, cayenne, and the remaining mint and ¼ teaspoon salt.

6. Serve the chops with the cucumber-mint salsa on the side.

LAMB SHISH KEBAB WITH YOGURT DIPPING SAUCE

SERVES 4

3 TABLESPOONS OLIVE OIL

¼ CUP PLUS 2 TABLESPOONS PLAIN
  LOW-FAT YOGURT

3 TABLESPOONS FRESH LEMON JUICE

2 GARLIC CLOVES, MINCED

1 TEASPOON OREGANO

¼ TEASPOON BLACK PEPPER

1 LARGE GREEN BELL PEPPER, CUT INTO
  1-INCH SQUARES

2 SMALL RED ONIONS, QUARTERED

1 POUND STEW LAMB, CUT INTO
  1-INCH PIECES

8 CHERRY TOMATOES

2 TABLESPOONS SOUR CREAM

1½ TEASPOONS GRATED LEMON ZEST

2 TABLESPOONS CHOPPED FRESH MINT,
  OR 1 TEASPOON DRIED

1. Preheat the broiler or prepare the grill. If broiling, line a broiler pan with foil.

2. In a small bowl, combine the oil, 2 tablespoons each of the yogurt and lemon juice, the garlic, oregano, and ⅛ teaspoon of the black pepper.

3. Thread the bell pepper, onions, lamb, and cherry tomatoes on 4 large or 8 small skewers. Brush the kebabs with half the garlic-yogurt basting mixture. Broil 4 inches from the heat for 3 minutes. Turn the kebabs over, brush

with the remaining basting mixture, and broil for 6 minutes, or until the lamb is medium-rare.

4. Meanwhile, in a small bowl, combine the sour cream, lemon zest, mint, and the remaining ¼ cup yogurt, 1 tablespoon lemon juice, the ⅛ teaspoon black pepper.

5. Serve the kebabs with the yogurt dipping sauce on the side.

Milanese Meatball Heros

SERVES 4

◆ EXTRA-QUICK

1 EGG WHITE

⅓ CUP (PACKED) PARSLEY SPRIGS, MINCED

2 TABLESPOONS TOMATO PASTE

2 TABLESPOONS FINE UNSEASONED DRY BREAD CRUMBS

3 GARLIC CLOVES, MINCED

1½ TEASPOONS OREGANO

¾ TEASPOON SALT

½ TEASPOON BLACK PEPPER

¼ TEASPOON RED PEPPER FLAKES

1 POUND GROUND VEAL

1 TABLESPOON OLIVE OIL

4 SMALL HERO ROLLS (ABOUT 4½ INCHES LONG) OR 2 LONG ROLLS (EACH ABOUT 9 INCHES LONG)

¼ CUP REDUCED-FAT MAYONNAISE

2 TABLESPOONS PLAIN LOW-FAT YOGURT

½ TEASPOON FRESH LEMON JUICE

2 TEASPOONS GRATED LEMON ZEST

2 MEDIUM TOMATOES, THINLY SLICED

1. Preheat the broiler.

2. In a medium bowl, lightly beat the egg white. Beat in 2 tablespoons of the parsley, the tomato paste, bread crumbs, 2 of the garlic cloves, the oregano, salt, black pepper, and red pepper flakes.

3. Add the veal to the egg-white mixture and mix until well blended. Form the mixture into 24 slightly flattened meatballs (about 1 heaping tablespoon each).

4. In a large nonstick skillet, warm the oil over medium-high heat. Add the meatballs and cook until well browned on the outside and medium-rare on the inside, about 6 min-

utes. Transfer the meatballs to a plate and cover loosely with foil to keep warm.

5. Meanwhile, split the rolls in half horizontally (if using long rolls, cut them in half crosswise first). Place them on a broiler pan and broil 4 inches from the heat until toasted, 30 seconds to 1 minute.

6. In a small bowl, combine the remaining parsley, 1 clove of garlic, the mayonnaise, yogurt, lemon juice, and lemon zest.

7. Spread the rolls lightly with the lemon-garlic mayonnaise. Top with the tomato slices. Place 6 meatballs in each sandwich.

VEAL PATTIES IN PARSLEY CREAM SAUCE

SERVES 4

◆ EXTRA-QUICK

1 EGG WHITE

1 MEDIUM ONION, FINELY CHOPPED

⅓ CUP (PACKED) PARSLEY SPRIGS,
    MINCED

½ POUND GROUND VEAL

⅔ CUP FINE UNSEASONED DRY BREAD
    CRUMBS

¾ CUP EVAPORATED MILK

½ TEASPOON NUTMEG

¼ TEASPOON ALLSPICE

¼ TEASPOON BLACK PEPPER

1 TABLESPOON OLIVE OIL

1 TABLESPOON FLOUR

1 CUP CHICKEN BROTH, PREFERABLY
    REDUCED-SODIUM

1. In a medium bowl, beat the egg white until frothy. Stir in the onion, half of the parsley, the veal, bread crumbs, ¼ cup of the evaporated milk, the nutmeg, allspice, and pepper. Form the mixture into 4 patties a scant ½ inch thick.

2. In a large nonstick skillet, warm the oil over medium-high heat. Add the patties and cook until browned, 3 to 4 minutes per side. Transfer the patties to a plate and cover loosely with foil to keep warm.

3. In a small bowl, combine the remaining ½ cup evaporated milk and the flour, and blend well.

4. Add the broth to the skillet and bring to a boil over medium-high heat, stirring to incorporate any browned bits clinging to the bottom of the pan. Stir in the flour-milk mixture and cook, stirring, until the sauce has thickened slightly, about 2 minutes.

5. Stir the remaining parsley into the skillet. Return the veal patties (and any juices that have collected on the plate) to the skillet and cook to coat the patties with the sauce and heat through, 1 to 2 minutes. Serve hot.

GRILLED BEEF AND AVOCADOS in FLOUR TORTILLAS

SERVES 4

♦ EXTRA-QUICK

2 TABLESPOONS UNSALTED BUTTER

2 TO 3 GARLIC CLOVES, MINCED

2 TABLESPOONS SWEET VERMOUTH

2 TABLESPOONS CHOPPED CILANTRO

2 POUNDS FLANK STEAK (¼ TO ½ INCH THICK)

2 LARGE AVOCADOS

¼ CUP FRESH LIME JUICE, PLUS 1 LIME CUT INTO WEDGES

¼ TEASPOON SALT

¼ TEASPOON BLACK PEPPER

8 FLOUR TORTILLAS, WRAPPED IN FOIL

1. Preheat the broiler or prepare the grill.

2. In a small saucepan, melt the butter over low heat. Add the garlic and cook until fragrant, about 1 minute. Remove the pan from the heat, add the vermouth and cilantro, and stir to combine.

3. Place the meat in a baking dish and, using your fingers, coat both sides of the meat with the vermouth-butter mixture.

4. Cut the avocados into 1½-inch chunks and place in a bowl. Add the lime juice and toss gently. Add the salt and pepper, and toss again.

5. Broil or grill the flank steak 4 inches from the heat for 6 to 8 minutes per side for medium-rare. Place the foil-wrapped tortillas on the side of the grill or in the oven to warm.

6. Cut the meat lengthwise into two pieces, then across the grain into ¼-inch-wide slices. Add the meat slices to the avocado and toss to combine.

7. Serve the beef and avocado with the flour tortillas and lime wedges.

GRILLED BEEF GYROS
WITH MIDDLE EASTERN SALAD

SERVES 4

¼ CUP FRESH LEMON JUICE

2 TABLESPOONS OLIVE OIL

2 GARLIC CLOVES, MINCED

1 TEASPOON OREGANO

½ PLUS ⅛ TEASPOON BLACK PEPPER

1 POUND FLANK STEAK

4 ROMAINE LETTUCE LEAVES, SHREDDED

1 MEDIUM CELERY RIB, FINELY CHOPPED

1 MEDIUM CARROT, FINELY CHOPPED

1 SMALL RED BELL PEPPER, FINELY CHOPPED

⅓ CUP REDUCED-FAT MAYONNAISE

⅓ CUP PLAIN LOW-FAT YOGURT

¼ CUP CHOPPED PARSLEY

2 TEASPOONS GRATED LEMON ZEST

½ TEASPOON SALT

4 PITA BREADS (ABOUT 6 INCHES IN DIAMETER)

1. Preheat the broiler or prepare the grill. If broiling, line a broiler pan with foil.

2. In a small bowl, combine 2 tablespoons of the lemon juice, the olive oil, garlic, oregano, and ⅛ teaspoon of the black pepper.

3. Brush half of the basting mixture on one side of the flank steak and broil or grill 4 inches from the heat for 8 minutes. Turn the steak over, brush with the remaining basting mixture, and broil or grill for 6 minutes for medium-rare. Set the steak aside on a plate to cool.

4. Meanwhile, place the lettuce, celery, carrot, and bell pepper in a medium bowl.

5. In a small bowl, combine the mayonnaise, yogurt, parsley, lemon zest, salt, and the remaining 2 tablespoons lemon juice and ½ teaspoon black pepper. Add ⅓ cup of the dressing to the vegetables and toss.

6. When ready to serve, thinly slice the steak on the diagonal. Cut the pita breads in half. Dividing evenly, stuff the pita breads with the salad. Top with slices of beef and some of the remaining dressing.

Light Fajita Roll-Ups

SERVES 4

◆ EXTRA-QUICK

3 TABLESPOONS CIDER VINEGAR

1 TEASPOON HONEY

1 TABLESPOON VEGETABLE OIL

3 GARLIC CLOVES, MINCED

2 TABLESPOONS CHILI POWDER

1 TABLESPOON CUMIN

¼ TEASPOON RED PEPPER FLAKES

1 POUND FLANK STEAK

1 LARGE ONION, HALVED LENGTHWISE
    THEN THINLY SLICED CROSSWISE

1 LARGE RED BELL PEPPER, CUT INTO
    THIN STRIPS

8 LARGE BOSTON OR BIBB LETTUCE
    LEAVES

¼ CUP PLAIN LOW-FAT YOGURT

1. In a shallow container large enough to hold the steak, combine the vinegar and honey, stirring until well blended. Blend in the oil, garlic, chili powder, cumin, and red pepper flakes. Add the flank steak to the marinade and turn to coat completely. Set aside.

2. Preheat the broiler. Line a broiler pan with foil.

3. Place the steak on the broiler pan, reserving the marinade. Broil 4 inches from the heat for 7 minutes. Turn the steak over and broil for 7 minutes, or until medium-rare. Set the steak aside for about 5 minutes before slicing; reserve the pan juices.

4. Meanwhile, transfer the reserved marinade to a medium skillet and warm over medium heat until bubbly. Add the onion and bell pepper, and cook for 1 to 2 minutes. Reduce the heat to low, cover, and cook until the vegetables are crisp-tender, about 6 minutes. Remove from the heat; when the steak is done, add the pan juices from the broiler pan to the onion-pepper mixture.

5. Thinly slice the steak across the grain. Dividing evenly, place the steak strips in the lettuce leaves. Add some of the onion-pepper mixture and ½ tablespoon of yogurt to each fajita. Serve 2 fajitas per person.

Beef Tacos with Fresh Salsa

SERVES 4

◆ EXTRA-QUICK

3 TABLESPOONS OLIVE OIL

1 SMALL ONION, COARSELY CHOPPED

2 GARLIC CLOVES, MINCED

½ POUND LEAN GROUND BEEF

HALF A 14½-OUNCE CAN NO-SALT-
ADDED STEWED TOMATOES, DRAINED

HALF A 4-OUNCE CAN OF CHOPPED
MILD GREEN CHILIES, DRAINED

2 TABLESPOONS CHILI POWDER

1½ TEASPOONS CUMIN

1 TEASPOON OREGANO

PINCH OF CAYENNE PEPPER

1 SMALL GREEN BELL PEPPER,
COARSELY CHOPPED

1 MEDIUM FRESH TOMATO, COARSELY
CHOPPED

3 SCALLIONS, COARSELY CHOPPED

¼ CUP CILANTRO SPRIGS, MINCED

2 TABLESPOONS RED WINE VINEGAR OR
CIDER VINEGAR

¼ TEASPOON BLACK PEPPER

3 DROPS OF HOT PEPPER SAUCE

12 TACO SHELLS

2 CUPS SHREDDED ROMAINE LETTUCE

1. In a large skillet, warm 1 tablespoon of the oil over medium-high heat. Add the onion and garlic, and cook until the mixture begins to brown, 3 to 5 minutes.

2. Crumble in the beef and cook for 2 to 3 minutes, breaking up the beef with a spoon.

3. Add the stewed tomatoes, green chilies, chili powder, cumin, ¼ teaspoon of the oregano, and the cayenne, breaking up the tomatoes with the back of a spoon. Reduce the heat to low, cover, and simmer while you prepare the remaining ingredients.

4. In a small bowl, combine the bell pepper, tomato, scallions, cilantro, vinegar, black pepper, hot pepper sauce, and the remaining 2 tablespoons oil and ¾ teaspoon oregano.

5. Fill each taco shell with ¼ cup of the beef mixture and top with shredded lettuce. Top the tacos with salsa or serve it on the side.

SLOPPY JOSÉS

SERVES 4

2 TEASPOONS VEGETABLE OIL

1 MEDIUM ONION, COARSELY CHOPPED

1 SMALL GREEN BELL PEPPER,
  COARSELY CHOPPED

3 GARLIC CLOVES, MINCED

1 POUND LEAN GROUND BEEF

⅔ CUP CHILI SAUCE

1 TABLESPOON TOMATO PASTE

2 TO 3 DROPS OF HOT PEPPER SAUCE,
  TO TASTE

1 TABLESPOON CHILI POWDER

1 TABLESPOON CUMIN

¼ TEASPOON SALT

¼ TEASPOON BLACK PEPPER

4 HAMBURGER BUNS, TOASTED

1. In a large skillet, warm the oil over medium-high heat. Add the onion, bell pepper, and garlic, and cook, stirring, until the onion begins to turn color, about 5 minutes.

2. Add the beef and cook for 5 minutes, stirring to break up the meat.

3. Add the chili sauce, tomato paste, hot pepper sauce, chili powder, cumin, salt, and black pepper. Bring to a boil, reduce the heat to medium-low, cover, and simmer 15 minutes.

4. Serve the sloppy Josés open-face over the toasted buns.

VARIATION: *It might be gilding the lily, but you could crown these South-of-the-Border sloppy joes with shredded cheese. Yellow or white Cheddar and Monterey jack or pepper jack cheese would all be good. But a truly authentic topping would be crumbly Mexican "queso blanco." To get close to the flavors of queso blanco without having to seek out the real thing (it's not widely available), you can use feta cheese. Just rinse it first to get rid of some of the salt.*

Spicy Oriental Hamburgers with Orange Sauce

SERVES 4

◆ EXTRA-QUICK

1 POUND LEAN GROUND BEEF

4 GARLIC CLOVES, MINCED

4 SCALLIONS, COARSELY CHOPPED

ONE 8-OUNCE CAN WHOLE OR SLICED
WATER CHESTNUTS, DRAINED AND
COARSELY CHOPPED

1¼ TEASPOONS GRATED ORANGE ZEST

¼ TEASPOON RED PEPPER FLAKES

1 TEASPOON VEGETABLE OIL

1 TEASPOON ORIENTAL (DARK) SESAME
OIL

¼ CUP FROZEN ORANGE JUICE
CONCENTRATE, THAWED

2 TABLESPOONS REDUCED-SODIUM SOY
SAUCE

1 TABLESPOON HONEY

1 TABLESPOON TOMATO PASTE

¼ TEASPOON BLACK PEPPER

¼ CUP CHICKEN BROTH BLENDED WITH
1 TEASPOON CORNSTARCH

1. In a medium bowl, combine the beef with half the garlic, half the scallions, all of the water chestnuts, the orange zest, and red pepper flakes. Form the mixture into 4 equal patties about ½ inch thick.

2. In a large skillet, warm the vegetable and sesame oils over medium-high heat. Add the hamburgers and cook for about 3 minutes per side for medium-rare, 4 minutes per side for medium, 5 minutes per side for well-done.

3. Transfer the hamburgers to a plate and cover loosely with foil to keep warm. Reduce the heat to medium and add the remaining garlic and scallions, the orange juice concentrate, soy sauce, honey, tomato paste, and black pepper. Bring to a boil. Stir the cornstarch mixture into the skillet and cook, stirring, until slightly thickened, 2 to 3 minutes.

4. Serve the hamburgers topped with some of the sauce.

Dijon Burgers
with Grilled Onions

SERVES 4

◆ EXTRA-QUICK

1 POUND LEAN GROUND BEEF

½ CUP FINE UNSEASONED DRY BREAD
CRUMBS

¼ CUP PLUS 2 TABLESPOONS DIJON
MUSTARD

¼ CUP DRY RED WINE

1 EGG

2 TEASPOONS TARRAGON

½ TEASPOON BLACK PEPPER

2 TABLESPOONS OLIVE OIL

1 LARGE RED ONION, CUT CROSSWISE
INTO 1-INCH-THICK SLICES

1 LARGE YELLOW ONION, CUT
CROSSWISE INTO 1-INCH-THICK
SLICES

1. Preheat the broiler or prepare the grill. If broiling, line a broiler pan with foil.

2. In a medium bowl, combine the beef, bread crumbs, 2 tablespoons of the mustard, 3 tablespoons of the red wine, the egg, 1 teaspoon of the tarragon, and ¼ teaspoon of the pepper. Form the meat mixture into 4 patties.

3. In a small bowl, combine the remaining ¼ cup mustard, 1 tablespoon red wine, 1 teaspoon tarragon, ¼ teaspoon pepper, and the oil, and whisk to blend well.

4. Brush the burgers and onion slices with half of the mustard mixture (if broiling, place them on the broiler pan first) and grill or broil 4 inches from the heat for 5 minutes.

5. Turn the burgers and onions over and brush with the remaining mustard mixture. Grill or broil for 4 minutes for medium-rare, 5 minutes for medium, 6 to 7 minutes for well-done.

HERBED STEAKBURGERS

SERVES 6 TO 8

1 CUP DARK BEER

1½ POUNDS LEAN STEAK, GROUND

½ POUND CARROTS OR PARSNIPS,
FINELY GRATED

1 SMALL ONION, FINELY CHOPPED

⅓ CUP FRESH WHOLE WHEAT BREAD
CRUMBS

2 TABLESPOONS CHOPPED PARSLEY

1 TABLESPOON GRAINY MUSTARD

2 TEASPOONS CHOPPED FRESH THYME,
OR ½ TEASPOON DRIED

½ TEASPOON SALT

¼ TEASPOON BLACK PEPPER

1. Preheat the broiler or prepare the grill. If broiling, line a broiler pan with foil.

2. In a small saucepan, bring the beer to a boil. Lower the heat and simmer until it has reduced to ¼ cup, about 5 minutes.

3. Place the ground steak in a large bowl and add the carrots, onion, bread crumbs, parsley, mustard, thyme, salt, and pepper. Pour in the beer. Using a wooden spoon, work the ingredients together until they are thoroughly combined.

4. Divide the mixture into 12 equal portions. Shape each portion into a ball, and flatten each ball into a patty.

5. Lightly oil the grill rack or the foil-lined broiler pan. Broil or grill the steakburgers 4 inches from the heat for 7 to 8 minutes per side for medium-rare.

KITCHEN NOTE: *Full-bodied bock beer would give robust flavor to these burgers: Brewed in the fall and aged through the winter, this German beer is the focus of festivals when it's ready for drinking in the spring. A dark malt liquor or stout are other good choices.*

Mexican Burgers
with Taco Toppings

SERVES 4

1½ POUNDS LEAN GROUND BEEF

2 SCALLIONS, THINLY SLICED

1½ TEASPOONS CHILI POWDER

1 TEASPOON FINELY MINCED PICKLED
    JALAPEÑO PEPPERS

½ TEASPOON SALT

½ TEASPOON BLACK PEPPER

4 ENGLISH MUFFINS, SPLIT

TACO TOPPINGS: BOTTLED SALSA,
    SHREDDED CHEDDAR CHEESE, DICED
    AVOCADO, SHREDDED LETTUCE,
    SLICED SCALLIONS

1. Prepare the grill.

2. In a medium bowl, combine the beef with the scallions, chili powder, jalapeños, and salt. Shape the meat into 4 patties about ¾ inch thick. Generously coat both sides of the patties with the black pepper.

3. Place the burgers on the grill and cook for 4 to 5 minutes per side for medium-rare, 5 to 6 minutes for medium, and 6 to 7 minutes for well-done. About 4 minutes before the burgers are done, place the muffins on the grill and toast on one side.

4. Serve the burgers with the toasted English muffins. Serve the taco toppings in individual bowls on the side.

Variation: *To make walk-around sandwiches for a backyard barbecue, substitute pita pockets for the English muffins. Make the burgers a bit flatter (about ½ inch thick); the cooking times will be a minute or so shorter. Wrap the pita breads in foil and heat them on the grill, then slice a sliver off the top edge of each pita, and put a burger in. Add salsa, shredded Cheddar, avocado, lettuce, and scallions to each sandwich.*

Mini-Beef Patties with Red Pepper Rice

SERVES 4

1 CUP RICE

1 LARGE RED BELL PEPPER, DICED

1 MEDIUM ONION, FINELY CHOPPED

1 POUND LEAN GROUND BEEF

⅓ CUP FINE UNSEASONED DRY BREAD CRUMBS

1 EGG

¼ CUP SPICY BROWN MUSTARD

1 TABLESPOON WORCESTERSHIRE SAUCE

1 TEASPOON OREGANO

½ TEASPOON BLACK PEPPER

2 TEASPOONS VEGETABLE OIL

3 TABLESPOONS UNSALTED BUTTER

½ POUND SMALL MUSHROOMS

2 TABLESPOONS FLOUR

1 CUP BEEF BROTH

½ CUP SOUR CREAM

1. In a medium saucepan, bring 2 cups of water to a boil. Add the rice, reduce the heat to medium-low, cover, and simmer until the rice is tender and all the liquid is absorbed, about 20 minutes. Five minutes before the rice is done, stir in the bell pepper.

2. Meanwhile, place half of the chopped onion in a medium bowl. Add the beef, bread crumbs, egg, 3 tablespoons of the mustard, the Worcestershire sauce, oregano, and ¼ teaspoon of the black pepper, and mix well. Form into 12 small patties ¼ inch thick.

3. In a large nonstick skillet, warm the oil over medium-high heat. Add the patties and cook until browned, about 3 minutes per side.

Transfer the patties to a plate and cover loosely with foil to keep warm.

4. Add the butter to the pan. Add the remaining onion and the mushrooms, and cook, stirring, until the mushrooms are just wilted, 2 to 3 minutes.

5. Blend in the flour, then stir in the broth, sour cream, the remaining 1 tablespoon mustard, and ¼ teaspoon black pepper. Bring the mixture to a boil and return the patties (and any juices that have collected on the plate) to the pan. Baste with some of the sauce and cook to heat through, about 1 minute.

6. Serve the patties topped with some of the sauce, and with the rice on the side.

STOVETOP BARBECUED BURGERS

SERVES 4

◆ EXTRA-QUICK

1 POUND LEAN GROUND BEEF

2 TEASPOONS OLIVE OIL

2 GARLIC CLOVES, MINCED

1 MEDIUM ONION, COARSELY CHOPPED

1 CUP CANNED CRUSHED TOMATOES

¼ CUP KETCHUP

2 TABLESPOONS FROZEN ORANGE JUICE
CONCENTRATE

1 TABLESPOON CHILI POWDER

¼ TEASPOON BLACK PEPPER

1. Form the beef into 4 even patties about 3½ inches in diameter and ¾ inch thick.

2. In a large skillet, warm the oil over medium-high heat until hot but not smoking. Add the burgers and cook for 5 minutes. Turn the burgers over and cook until browned on the second side but still slightly pink in the center, about 4 minutes. Transfer the burgers to a plate and cover loosely with foil to keep warm.

3. Add the garlic and onion to the skillet and cook, stirring, over medium heat until the onion begins to brown, about 5 minutes.

4. Add the tomatoes, ketchup, orange juice concentrate, chili powder, and pepper. Bring the mixture to a boil over medium-high heat and boil for 1 minute.

5. Return the burgers (and any juices that have collected on the plate) to the skillet, baste with the sauce, and cook until the burgers are heated through, about 1 minute.

KITCHEN NOTE: *For the leanest burgers, buy ground sirloin or ground round. Or look for extra-lean ground beef, usually labeled "10 percent," indicating that the meat is 10 percent fat by weight. Beware, however, of meat simply labeled "ground beef," as it can be as much as 30 percent fat by weight (which is responsible for 75 percent or more of the calories).*

Lamb Burgers with Basil and Parmesan Sauce

SERVES 8

1½ POUNDS LEAN LEG OF LAMB, GROUND

3 ONIONS, CHOPPED

½ POUND ZUCCHINI, COARSELY GRATED

⅔ CUP FRESH WHOLE WHEAT BREAD CRUMBS

¼ TEASPOON SALT

¼ TEASPOON BLACK PEPPER

½ TEASPOON OLIVE OIL

⅔ CUP CHICKEN BROTH, PREFERABLY REDUCED-SODIUM

½ CUP (LOOSELY PACKED) FRESH BASIL LEAVES, COARSELY CHOPPED

¼ CUP GRATED PARMESAN CHEESE

1. Prepare the grill.

2. Put the ground lamb into a bowl. Add one-third of the chopped onion, all of the zucchini, the bread crumbs, salt, and pepper, and thoroughly combine. Divide the mixture into 16 equal portions, then shape each portion into a patty about 2½ inches in diameter and ½ inch thick. Place the burgers on a baking sheet and set them aside.

3. In a small saucepan, warm the oil over medium heat. Add the remaining chopped onions and cook them gently until they begin to soften, about 3 minutes.

4. Pour the broth into the pan and bring it to a boil. Cover the pan, lower the heat, and simmer the sauce until the onion is tender, 4 to 5 minutes.

5. Stir in the basil and cheese, and cook the sauce for 1 minute. Transfer the sauce to a food processor or blender and process it until it is smooth. Pour the sauce back into the saucepan and set it aside, ready to be reheated very gently just before serving.

6. Lightly oil the grill rack and cook the burgers 4 inches from the heat for 7 to 8 minutes per side. Serve two burgers per person, with a little of the reheated sauce.

HERBED PORK BURGERS WITH APPLE-CARROT RELISH

SERVES 4

1 POUND LEAN GROUND PORK

1 TEASPOON SAGE

½ TEASPOON FENNEL SEEDS

1 TEASPOON SALT

¾ TEASPOON BLACK PEPPER

1 TEASPOON OLIVE OIL

2 GARLIC CLOVES, MINCED

1 MEDIUM ONION, COARSELY CHOPPED

3 MEDIUM CARROTS, SHREDDED

2 MEDIUM UNPEELED APPLES,
   COARSELY CHOPPED

2 TABLESPOONS BEEF BROTH

2 TABLESPOONS CIDER VINEGAR

2 TEASPOONS SUGAR

1. In a medium bowl, blend the pork, sage, fennel seeds, ½ teaspoon each of the salt and pepper. Form the mixture into 4 patties a scant ½ inch thick.

2. In a large nonstick skillet, warm the oil over medium-high heat. Add the patties and cook until golden brown on both sides and no longer pink in the middle, 6 to 7 minutes per side. Transfer the burgers to a plate and place in a low oven to keep warm.

3. Add the garlic and onion to the skillet and stir-fry until the onion begins to turn brown, 3 to 5 minutes.

4. Add the carrots, apples, broth, vinegar, sugar, and remaining ½ teaspoon salt and ¼ teaspoon pepper. Cook, stirring, over medium-high heat until the carrots are tender, about 10 minutes.

5. Serve burgers with the apple-carrot relish on the side.

CHILI-TOPPED PORK BURGERS

SERVES 4

½ POUND PORK TENDERLOIN, GROUND
   OR VERY FINELY CHOPPED

½ POUND VEAL ROUND, GROUND OR
   VERY FINELY CHOPPED

1 ONION, VERY FINELY CHOPPED

¼ TEASPOON SALT

½ TEASPOON DRY MUSTARD

¼ TEASPOON CHILI POWDER

1 TABLESPOON OLIVE OIL

¼ CUP CHILI RELISH

1 CARROT, GRATED

2 SHALLOTS, FINELY CHOPPED

1-INCH PIECE OF CUCUMBER, FINELY
   CHOPPED

4 CRISP LETTUCE LEAVES

4 SLICES OF TOMATO

4 HAMBURGER BUNS, TOASTED

1. In a bowl, mix the pork with the veal, onion, salt, mustard, and chili powder. Form the mixture into 4 patties about ½ inch thick.

2. In a large skillet, warm the oil over medium heat. Add the burgers and cook until browned and cooked through, about 6 minutes per side.

3. Meanwhile, in a bowl, mix the chili relish with the carrot, shallots, and cucumber.

4. Arrange a lettuce leaf on the bottom portion of each bun, then add a burger to each, and top with a slice of tomato and a spoonful of chili topping. Cover with the bun tops and secure them in position with cocktail sticks.

Substitution: *Use ground turkey instead of veal. Rather than buying a package of already ground turkey (which may contain dark meat and fatty skin), choose a piece of turkey breast and have the butcher grind it without the skin. Or, grind the turkey at home: Cut it into chunks and chop them in your food processor.*

Mexican Steak Salad

SERVES 4

1 LARGE AVOCADO

¼ CUP CHOPPED SCALLIONS

1 TEASPOON FRESH LIME JUICE

¾ TEASPOON SALT

2 GARLIC CLOVES, MINCED

¼ CUP PLUS 2 TEASPOONS OLIVE OIL

1½ POUNDS SIRLOIN TIP, TOP SIRLOIN,
   OR FLANK STEAK

½ TEASPOON CRACKED BLACK PEPPER

2 TABLESPOONS WHITE WINE VINEGAR

¼ TEASPOON OREGANO

PINCH OF CUMIN

8 CUPS SHREDDED ICEBERG LETTUCE

½ CUP SOUR CREAM

2 OUNCES SHREDDED MONTEREY JACK
   CHEESE

2 OUNCES SHREDDED CHEDDAR CHEESE

2 MEDIUM TOMATOES, CUT INTO
   ½-INCH DICE

3 CUPS UNSALTED TORTILLA CHIPS

1. Halve the avocado and scoop the flesh into a medium bowl. Mash the avocado with a fork, then add the scallions, lime juice, and ⅛ teaspoon of the salt. Cover with plastic wrap and refrigerate.

2. Preheat the broiler. Line a broiler pan with foil.

3. In a small bowl, mash the garlic and ½ teaspoon salt with the back of a spoon to form a paste. Drizzle 1 teaspoon of the oil over one side of the steak and evenly spread with half the garlic paste and ¼ teaspoon of the pepper. Turn the steak over and repeat on the other side.

4. Broil the meat 5 inches from the heat for 5 minutes. Turn meat over and broil for 3 min-

utes for medium-rare. Transfer the steak to a cutting board. Cut into ½-inch-thick strips and then cut the strips crosswise into ½-inch cubes.

5. Meanwhile, in a small bowl or small screwtop jar, combine the remaining ¼ cup oil with the vinegar, oregano, cumin, and remaining ⅛ teaspoon salt, and blend well.

6. Toss the lettuce with the dressing and divide among 4 dinner plates. Top the lettuce with the steak. Place a dollop of sour cream and a dollop of avocado mixture next to each other on top of the steak. Sprinkle with the shredded cheeses and top with diced tomato. Arrange a border of tortilla chips on the rim of each plate and serve.

Marinated Beef Salad

SERVES 4 TO 6

¼ CUP VEGETABLE OIL, PREFERABLY
    PEANUT OIL

1 TEASPOON ORIENTAL (DARK) SESAME
    OIL

1-INCH PIECE OF FRESH GINGER,
    MINCED

1½ TABLESPOONS CHOPPED CILANTRO
    OR PARSLEY

1½ TABLESPOONS CHOPPED FRESH
    MINT, OR 1 TEASPOON DRIED

2 TEASPOONS GRATED LIME ZEST

½ TEASPOON SALT

1½ POUNDS SLICED ROAST BEEF, CUT
    INTO ¼-INCH-WIDE STRIPS

2 SMALL CANTALOUPES (½ TO ¾
    POUND EACH), PEELED AND THINLY
    SLICED

1 LARGE HEAD OF ROMAINE LETTUCE,
    SHREDDED

¼ CUP FRESH LIME JUICE PLUS 1 LIME,
    CUT INTO 8 WEDGES

1 TABLESPOON SESAME SEEDS

RED PEPPER FLAKES, TO TASTE

1. In a small bowl, combine the vegetable oil, sesame oil, ginger, cilantro, mint, lime zest, and salt.

2. In a medium bowl, toss the roast beef with the dressing, cover loosely, and refrigerate until chilled.

3. Arrange the cantaloupe slices around the edge of a serving platter. Form a bed of lettuce in the center. Toss the meat mixture again and then spoon over the lettuce. Sprinkle the melon and the salad with the lime juice.

4. Just before serving, top with sesame seeds and sprinkle lightly with red pepper flakes. Serve the lime wedges and additional red pepper flakes on the side.

BEEF AND TOMATO SALAD

SERVES 4

1 TABLESPOON OLIVE OIL

1 POUND FLANK STEAK, CUT WITH THE
  GRAIN INTO 2 STRIPS, THEN ACROSS
  THE GRAIN INTO THIN SLICES

1 TABLESPOON CHOPPED FRESH BASIL,
  OR 1 TEASPOON DRIED

1 POUND TOMATOES, CUT INTO
  ½-INCH DICE

4 ROMAINE LETTUCE LEAVES

½ CUP SOUR CREAM, AT ROOM
  TEMPERATURE

¾ CUP THINLY SLICED SCALLIONS

½ CUP FINELY CHOPPED PARSLEY

¼ TEASPOON SALT

¼ TEASPOON BLACK PEPPER

1. In large skillet, warm the oil over medium-high heat. Add the beef and basil, and stir-fry just until the meat is no longer pink, about 2 minutes. Add the tomatoes and stir-fry until they are just warm, about 1 minute.

2. Line a serving platter with the lettuce. Spoon the beef-tomato mixture on top. Top with the sour cream, scallions, and parsley. Season with the salt and pepper, and toss gently to combine.

VARIATION: *For a heartier meal, put on a pot of ziti or penne to cook while you slice and stir-fry the steak and tomatoes. Drain the pasta well, toss it with the sour cream, scallions, and parsley, then add the tomatoes, beef, salt, and pepper, and toss gently. Serve with a salad of Romaine and thinly sliced Bermuda onions.*

THAI GRILLED BEEF SALAD

SERVES 4

2 4 TEASPOONS MINCED FRESH GINGER

¼ CUP PLUS 2 TABLESPOONS
VEGETABLE OIL

2 TABLESPOONS REDUCED-SODIUM SOY
SAUCE

3 GARLIC CLOVES, MINCED

2 TEASPOONS GRANULATED SUGAR

¼ TEASPOON BLACK PEPPER

1¼ POUNDS FLANK STEAK

¼ CUP (PACKED) FRESH MINT LEAVES,
OR 2 TEASPOONS DRIED

¼ CUP FRESH LEMON JUICE

3 TABLESPOONS FRESH LIME JUICE

1 TEASPOON GRATED LIME ZEST

2 DROPS OF HOT PEPPER SAUCE

1 TABLESPOON ANCHOVY PASTE

1 TABLESPOON BROWN SUGAR

3 PLUM TOMATOES, CUT INTO BITE-
SIZE PIECES

1 SMALL CUCUMBER, CUT INTO BITE-
SIZE PIECES

3 SCALLIONS, COARSELY CHOPPED

3 CUPS SHREDDED ICEBERG LETTUCE (CABBAGE)

¼ POUND BEAN SPROUTS

2 TEASPOONS SESAME SEEDS

1. Preheat the broiler or prepare the grill. If broiling, line a broiler pan with foil.

2. In a small bowl, combine 2 teaspoons of the ginger with 2 tablespoons of the oil, the soy sauce, 2 of the garlic cloves, the granulated sugar, and pepper.

3. Brush the steak with half of the ginger basting mixture and grill or broil 4 inches from the heat for 4 minutes. Turn the steak over, brush with the remaining ginger basting mixture and cook another 5 minutes for rare, 6 minutes for medium-rare, 7 minutes for medium. Let the steak stand for 5 minutes before slicing.

4. Meanwhile, in a food processor, mince the fresh mint (if using). Add the lemon and lime juices, lime zest, hot pepper sauce, anchovy paste, brown sugar, and the remaining minced ginger, garlic, and ¼ cup oil. (If using dried mint, add here.) Process to blend.

5. In a large bowl, toss the tomatoes, cucumber, scallions, lettuce and sprouts together.

6. Cut the steak with the grain into strips, then cut the strips crosswise into thin slices. Arrange the vegetables on individual dinner plates. Top with steak slices, dressing, and sesame seeds.

BEEF AND BARLEY
SALAD WITH CHERRY TOMATOES

SERVES 4

½ CUP PEARL BARLEY

2 CUPS BEEF BROTH, PREFERABLY
REDUCED-SODIUM

3 TABLESPOONS FRESH LEMON JUICE

2 TABLESPOONS RED WINE VINEGAR OR
CIDER VINEGAR

2 TABLESPOONS OLIVE OIL

2 TABLESPOONS DIJON MUSTARD

2 TEASPOONS GRATED LEMON ZEST

½ TEASPOON BROWN SUGAR

½ TEASPOON BLACK PEPPER

1 PINT CHERRY TOMATOES, QUARTERED

4 SCALLIONS, COARSELY CHOPPED

½ POUND SLICED ROAST BEEF, CUT
INTO THIN STRIPS

½ CUP RAISINS

1. In a medium saucepan, combine the barley and beef broth, and bring to a boil over high heat. Reduce the heat to low, cover, and simmer until the barley is just tender, about 50 minutes.

2. Meanwhile, in a small saucepan or skillet, combine the lemon juice, vinegar, oil, mustard, lemon zest, sugar, and pepper. Cook over medium heat until just heated through, 3 to 4 minutes.

3. In a serving bowl, combine the tomatoes, scallions, roast beef, and raisins. Pour the dressing over the vegetables and roast beef, and toss to combine. Set aside until the barley is done.

4. Add the hot barley to the serving bowl and stir to combine. Serve the salad warm, at room temperature, or chilled.

PORK AND GINGER STIR-FRY SALAD

SERVES 4

1 TABLESPOON ORIENTAL (DARK) SESAME OIL

1 GARLIC CLOVE, MINCED

1-INCH PIECE FRESH GINGER, FINELY CHOPPED

1 TEASPOON CHILI SAUCE

2 TABLESPOONS REDUCED-SODIUM SOY SAUCE

3 SHALLOTS, THINLY SLICED

⅛ TEASPOON CHINESE 5-SPICE POWDER (OPTIONAL)

1 POUND PORK TENDERLOIN, CUT INTO THIN STRIPS

½ SMALL HEAD RED LEAF LETTUCE, SEPARATED INTO LEAVES

6 CURLY ENDIVE LEAVES

1 BUNCH OF WATERCRESS, STEMS TRIMMED

4 NAPA CABBAGE LEAVES, SHREDDED

4 SCALLIONS, SLICED DIAGONALLY

1 CUP BEAN SPROUTS

1 TABLESPOON OLIVE OIL

1 RED BELL PEPPER, CUT INTO THIN STRIPS

1. In a large bowl, mix the sesame oil with the garlic, ginger, chili sauce, soy sauce, shallots, and 5-spice powder (if using). Add the pork strips and mix well. Cover and marinate for at least 15 minutes.

2. Meanwhile, arrange the lettuce, curly endive leaves, and watercress sprigs in a border around a serving dish. Mix the shredded napa cabbage with the scallions and bean sprouts, and place the mixture in the center of the dish.

3. In a wok or large skillet, warm the olive oil over medium-high heat. Add the pork and its marinade, and cook for 4 minutes, stirring all the time. Add the bell pepper strips and cook for 1 to 2 minutes, stirring constantly.

4. Pile the hot pork mixture over the salad and serve at once.

WARM LENTIL AND SAUSAGE SALAD

SERVES 4

½ POUND CHORIZO OR PEPPERONI

1 CUP LENTILS, RINSED AND PICKED OVER

½ CUP CHOPPED ONION

½ TEASPOON SALT

1 BAY LEAF

½ CUP VEGETABLE OIL

2 TABLESPOONS FRESH LEMON JUICE

2 TABLESPOONS RED WINE VINEGAR

¼ TEASPOON MINCED GARLIC

¼ TEASPOON CUMIN

¼ TEASPOON HOT PEPPER SAUCE

¼ CUP MINCED PARSLEY

1 BUNCH OF WATERCRESS, STEMS TRIMMED

1 SMALL RED ONION, THINLY SLICED

1. Remove casing from chorizo and cut the sausage into 1½ x ½-inch strips. In a small nonstick skillet, sauté the chorizo until lightly browned, about 5 minutes. Transfer the chorizo to paper towels to drain.

2. In a large saucepan, combine the lentils, onion, salt, bay leaf, and 1 quart cold water, and bring to a boil over high heat. Reduce the heat to medium, cover, and simmer gently until the lentils are tender, 15 to 17 minutes. Drain the lentils and discard the bay leaf.

Place the lentils in a serving bowl and cover loosely to keep warm.

3. Meanwhile, in a small bowl, combine the oil, lemon juice, vinegar, garlic, cumin, and hot pepper sauce, and stir to blend.

4. Just before serving, add the sausage to the lentils. Pour the dressing over the salad and toss. Divide the salad among 4 dinner plates and sprinkle with parsley. Top with watercress and red onion slices, and serve.

KITCHEN NOTE: *Watercress has a lot to offer: Its attractive dark-green leaves have a wonderfully peppery flavor, and it's an excellent source of vitamin C and beta carotene. Choose a crisp, fresh-looking bunch of watercress; to wash it, hold the bunch by the stems and swish the leaves vigorously in a basin of water.*

BEEF AND MUSHROOM SOUP

SERVES 6

1 OUNCE DRIED MUSHROOMS

2 CUPS BOILING WATER

6 CUPS REDUCED-SODIUM CHICKEN
   BROTH

2 TABLESPOONS OLIVE OIL

1 POUND TOP SIRLOIN, CUT INTO
   ½-INCH-WIDE STRIPS

5 GARLIC CLOVES, MINCED

1 LARGE ONION, FINELY CHOPPED

1 POUND FRESH MUSHROOMS, SLICED

½ TEASPOON SALT

½ CUP DRY SHERRY OR MARSALA

2 TABLESPOONS REDUCED-SODIUM SOY
   SAUCE

¼ TEASPOON BLACK PEPPER

2 TABLESPOONS CHOPPED PARSLEY

1. In a heatproof bowl, combine the mushrooms and boiling water, and set aside to soak until softened, about 10 minutes. Reserving the soaking liquid, cut off and discard the mushroom stems. Thinly slice the caps and set aside. Gradually pour the mushroom soaking liquid into a large pot, carefully leaving any grit behind. Discard the gritty liquid. Add the broth to the pot and bring the liquid to a simmer.

2. Meanwhile, in a large skillet, warm 1 tablespoon of the oil over medium-high heat. Add the beef and cook, stirring frequently, until browned, about 2 minutes. Transfer the beef to a plate and set aside.

3. Warm the remaining 1 tablespoon oil in the skillet over medium-high heat. Add the garlic and onion, and stir-fry for 30 seconds. Stir in the soaked and fresh mushrooms and ¼ teaspoon of the salt, and cook, stirring frequently, for 5 minutes.

4. Pour in the sherry and stir to scrape up any browned bits clinging to the bottom of the pan. Add the contents of the skillet to the simmering broth along with the soy sauce, pepper, and remaining ¼ teaspoon salt. Simmer the soup, stirring occasionally, for 20 minutes.

5. Stir in the sautéed beef and cook until heated through, about 1 minute. Garnish the soup with the parsley and serve hot.

EASY VEAL STEW

SERVES 4

2 TABLESPOONS OLIVE OIL

3 SLICES BACON, CUT CROSSWISE INTO
¼-INCH-WIDE STRIPS

1 MEDIUM ONION, COARSELY CHOPPED

1 CELERY RIB WITH LEAVES, DICED

1 GARLIC CLOVE, MINCED

1 BAY LEAF

ONE 16-OUNCE CAN NO-SALT-ADDED
WHOLE TOMATOES

2 POUNDS VEAL STEW MEAT, CUT INTO
1-INCH CUBES

½ CUP DRY WHITE WINE

½ TEASPOON SALT

¼ TEASPOON BLACK PEPPER

1. In a large nonstick skillet, warm the oil over medium-high heat. Add the bacon and cook, stirring frequently, until lightly browned, about 4 minutes.

2. Stir in the onion, celery, garlic, and bay leaf. Cover, reduce the heat to very low, and cook, stirring often, until the vegetables are softened but not browned, about 15 minutes.

3. Stir in the tomatoes, veal, and wine, breaking up the tomatoes with the back of a spoon. Increase the heat to high and cook, stirring constantly, until the liquid comes to a boil. Reduce the heat to low, cover, and simmer until the veal is tender, about 45 minutes.

4. Stir in the salt and pepper, and remove the bay leaf. Serve hot.

SUBSTITUTION: *If you'd rather not cook with wine—or don't happen to have any on hand—you can substitute chicken broth. Or, for a tangy flavor, try apple juice or apple cider.*

CHILI WITH NO BEANS

SERVES 4 TO 6

3 POUNDS TOP SIRLOIN, CUT INTO
  ½-INCH CUBES
3 GARLIC CLOVES, MINCED
¼ CUP CHILI POWDER
2 TEASPOONS CUMIN
2 TEASPOONS OREGANO
¾ TEASPOON SALT

2 TABLESPOONS UNSALTED BUTTER
1 LARGE ONION, COARSELY CHOPPED
2 CUPS BEER OR DRY RED WINE
½ CUP SHREDDED MONTEREY JACK
  CHEESE
½ CUP SHREDDED CHEDDAR CHEESE

1. In a large bowl, combine the meat with the garlic, chili powder, cumin, oregano, and salt. Toss to coat and set aside.

2. In a large saucepan, warm the butter over medium heat until melted. Add the onion and cook, stirring frequently, until translucent, about 5 minutes.

3. Stir in one-fourth of the meat, increase the heat to medium-high, and cook, stirring, until the meat is lightly browned and encrusted with spices, about 3 minutes. Transfer to a platter. Add the remaining meat to the pan and cook until lightly browned.

4. Meanwhile, in a small saucepan, bring the beer and 2 cups of water to a boil over medium-high heat.

5. Return all the meat to the saucepan, add the hot beer mixture, and stir to combine. Reduce the heat to low and cook until the meat is tender and the liquid is reduced to a sauce, about 15 minutes. (If the sauce is not thick enough, transfer the meat to a serving bowl and boil the liquid in the pan to reduce it. Then pour the reduced liquid over the meat in the bowl.)

6. Serve the chili topped with the two cheeses.

CHUCKWAGON BEEF STEW WITH DUMPLINGS

SERVES 4

◇ LOW - FAT

1 TABLESPOON OLIVE OIL

1 POUND BEEF ROUND, CUT INTO
   ½-INCH CUBES

2 GARLIC CLOVES, FINELY CHOPPED

2 CUPS CHICKEN BROTH, PREFERABLY
   REDUCED-SODIUM

1 LARGE ONION, CUT INTO ¾-INCH
   CUBES

1 LARGE GREEN BELL PEPPER, CUT INTO
   ¾-INCH SQUARES

½ CUP RICE

¼ TEASPOON CUMIN

⅜ TEASPOON SALT

⅛ TEASPOON CAYENNE PEPPER

1 CUP CORNMEAL

1¼ TEASPOONS BAKING POWDER

1 CUP LOW-FAT MILK

2 TABLESPOONS CHOPPED CILANTRO OR
   PARSLEY

2 EARS OF CORN, EACH CUT INTO
   4 PIECES

1 LARGE TOMATO, COARSELY CHOPPED

1. In a large nonstick skillet, warm 1 teaspoon of the oil over medium-high heat. Add the beef and cook, stirring frequently, until browned, about 1 minute. Add the garlic and cook, stirring constantly, for 1 minute.

2. Reduce the heat to medium and stir in the broth, 2 cups of water, the onion, bell pepper, rice, cumin, ½ teaspoon of the salt, and the cayenne. Bring the liquid to a simmer, cover, and cook until the rice is tender, about 20 minutes.

3. Meanwhile, in a medium bowl, combine the cornmeal, baking powder, and remaining

⅛ teaspoon salt. Stir in the remaining 2 teaspoons oil, then pour in the milk, stirring until a thick batter forms. Stir in the cilantro and set the dumpling batter aside while the stew is cooking.

4. Add the corn and tomato to the stew and return the mixture to a simmer. Drop large spoonfuls of the batter onto the stew, cover, and simmer until the dumplings are cooked through, 12 to 15 minutes. Serve hot.

THREE-PEPPER SMOTHERED MINUTE STEAK

SERVES 4

◆ EXTRA-QUICK

½ CUP BEEF BROTH

2 GARLIC CLOVES, MINCED

1 TEASPOON OREGANO

¼ TEASPOON BLACK PEPPER

1 MEDIUM RED BELL PEPPER, CUT INTO THIN STRIPS

1 MEDIUM YELLOW BELL PEPPER, CUT INTO THIN STRIPS

1 MEDIUM GREEN BELL PEPPER, CUT INTO THIN STRIPS

1 SMALL ONION, THINLY SLICED

1 TABLESPOON OLIVE OIL

1 MINUTE STEAK (ABOUT ¾ POUND)

1 TABLESPOON CORNSTARCH BLENDED WITH 2 TABLESPOONS WATER

1. In a medium saucepan, bring the broth, garlic, oregano, and black pepper to a boil over medium-high heat. Add the bell peppers and onion. Return to a boil, reduce the heat to low, cover, and simmer for 5 minutes.

2. Meanwhile, in a medium nonstick skillet, warm the oil over medium-high heat. Add the steak and cook until browned, about 3 minutes per side. Transfer to a plate and cover loosely with foil to keep warm.

3. Return the pepper-onion mixture to a boil over medium-high heat, stir in the cornstarch mixture, and cook, stirring constantly, until the mixture thickens slightly, about 1 minute.

4. Cut the steak into serving portions and serve topped with the peppers and onion.

SAUSAGES PIZZAIOLA

SERVES 4

4 SWEET ITALIAN SAUSAGES (ABOUT
  1 POUND TOTAL)
4 HOT ITALIAN SAUSAGES (ABOUT
  1 POUND TOTAL)
2 TABLESPOONS OLIVE OIL
3 GARLIC CLOVES, LIGHTLY CRUSHED
  AND PEELED

TWO 16-OUNCE CANS CRUSHED
  TOMATOES
1 TEASPOON OREGANO
1 TEASPOON SALT
¼ TEASPOON RED PEPPER FLAKES

1. Prick the sausages in several places with the tip of a sharp knife. In a large skillet, combine the sausages with enough water to cover. Bring the water to a boil over high heat, reduce the heat to low, and simmer the sausages for 15 minutes.

2. Meanwhile, in a large saucepan, warm the oil over medium heat. Add the garlic and cook, stirring frequently, until softened, about 3 minutes; do not brown.

3. Stir in the tomatoes, oregano, salt, and red pepper flakes, and simmer, stirring occasionally, until the flavors are blended, about 10 minutes.

4. Drain the sausages and transfer them to the sauce. Return to a simmer and cook, stirring occasionally, until the mixture is slightly thickened, about 15 minutes.

5. Serve the sausages with the sauce spooned on top.

SWEET AFTERTHOUGHT: *Cap this rich, highly seasoned Italian-style meal with scoops of raspberry ice or sorbet sprinkled with very finely grated bittersweet chocolate. Accompany this cool dessert with Italian-roast coffee, either hot or iced.*

Simple Beef Burgundy

SERVES 4

◆ EXTRA-QUICK

1 POUND FLANK STEAK, CUT WITH THE
    GRAIN INTO 2 STRIPS, THEN ACROSS
    THE GRAIN INTO THIN SLICES
½ CUP DRY RED WINE
3 TABLESPOONS UNSALTED BUTTER
2 GARLIC CLOVES, MINCED
½ POUND MUSHROOMS, THINLY SLICED
8 SCALLIONS, CUT INTO 2-INCH
    LENGTHS

2 TABLESPOONS FLOUR
½ TEASPOON SALT
¼ TEASPOON BLACK PEPPER
¼ CUP BEEF BROTH
1 TEASPOON TARRAGON
¼ CUP CHOPPED PARSLEY (OPTIONAL)

1. In a medium bowl, combine the steak and wine, and let marinate at room temperature while you prepare the vegetables.

2. In a large nonstick skillet, warm 1 tablespoon of the butter over medium heat until melted. Add the garlic, mushrooms, and scallions, and cook, stirring frequently, until the mushrooms have softened, about 5 minutes. Transfer to a bowl and set aside.

3. In a plastic or paper bag, combine the flour, salt, and pepper. Reserving the marinade, drain the beef in a colander or strainer. Place the drained beef in the bag of seasoned flour and shake to coat.

4. Wipe the skillet clean. Add the remaining 2 tablespoons butter to the skillet and warm over medium-high heat until melted. Add the dredged beef and stir-fry until browned, about 3 minutes.

5. Return the sautéed vegetables with any liquid to the pan. Stir in the reserved marinade, the broth, and tarragon. Bring to a boil and cook, stirring constantly, until the mixture is slightly thickened, 1 to 2 minutes.

6. Serve the beef burgundy hot, sprinkled with the parsley if desired.

PORK CHOPS WITH FRESH CRANBERRY SAUCE

SERVES 4

♦ EXTRA-QUICK

3 TABLESPOONS FLOUR

¼ TEASPOON BLACK PEPPER

4 CENTER-CUT LOIN PORK CHOPS
(½ INCH THICK, ABOUT 1¼ POUNDS
TOTAL)

1 TABLESPOON VEGETABLE OIL

1 TABLESPOON UNSALTED BUTTER

½ CUP APPLE JUICE

½ CUP CHICKEN BROTH

1 TABLESPOON BROWN SUGAR

1 TABLESPOON GRATED ORANGE ZEST

1 CUP CRANBERRIES, FRESH OR FROZEN

2 SCALLIONS, COARSELY CHOPPED

1. In a shallow bowl, combine the flour and pepper. Lightly dredge the pork chops in the seasoned flour; reserve 1 tablespoon of the excess seasoned flour.

2. In a large skillet, warm the oil over medium-high heat. Add the chops and cook until browned, 2 to 3 minutes per side. Transfer the chops to a plate and cover loosely with foil to keep warm.

3. Add the butter to the skillet and melt over medium heat. Add the reserved 1 tablespoon seasoned flour and stir until the flour has absorbed all of the butter, about 30 seconds.

4. Stir in the apple juice, broth, brown sugar, and zest. Add the cranberries and bring the mixture to a boil over medium-high heat.

5. Return the pork chops (and any juices that have collected on the plate) to the skillet, reduce the heat to medium-low, cover, and simmer for 5 minutes. Turn the chops over, cover, and simmer until they are cooked through and the sauce is slightly thickened, about 5 minutes.

6. Stir the scallions into the sauce and serve the chops with some of the cranberry sauce spooned over them.

ROAST EYE ROUND WITH MUSHROOM SAUCE

SERVES 8

¼ CUP CRACKED BLACK PEPPERCORNS

2½ TABLESPOONS DIJON MUSTARD

2 TABLESPOONS PLAIN LOW-FAT YOGURT

2½ POUNDS EYE ROUND ROAST

2 TABLESPOONS OLIVE OIL

½ POUND SMALL MUSHROOMS, QUARTERED

⅓ CUP THINLY SLICED SHALLOTS OR CHOPPED ONIONS

1 TABLESPOON CHOPPED FRESH ROSEMARY, OR ¾ TEASPOON DRIED

1 CUP DRY RED WINE

1 GARLIC CLOVE, MINCED

2 CUPS BEEF OR CHICKEN BROTH, PREFERABLY REDUCED-SODIUM

¼ TEASPOON SALT

¼ CUP HALF-AND-HALF

1 TABLESPOON CORNSTARCH

1. Preheat the oven to 500°.

2. Spread the cracked peppercorns on a plate. In a cup, stir together 2 tablespoons of the mustard and the yogurt, and smear this mixture over the beef. Roll the beef in the peppercorns, coating evenly on all sides.

3. Place the beef on a rack in a roasting pan and roast for 35 minutes, or until a meat thermometer inserted in the center registers 140° for medium-rare. Let the roast stand while you prepare the mushroom sauce.

4. In a large skillet, warm the oil over medium heat. Add the mushrooms, shallots, and rosemary, and cook, stirring frequently, for 5 minutes. Add the wine and garlic, increase the heat to high, and boil rapidly until the liquid is reduced by half, about 3 minutes. Stir in the broth and salt, and boil until the liquid is reduced to about 1¼ cups.

5. In a cup, combine the half-and-half and cornstarch, stir to blend, and whisk into the boiling mushroom mixture along with the remaining 1½ teaspoons mustard. Reduce the heat to medium and cook, whisking constantly, until the sauce is slightly thickened, about 1 minute. Remove from the heat.

6. To serve, carve the roast into very thin slices. Arrange the slices on a platter and pour the mushroom sauce over them.

Maple-Glazed Pork Chops with Roasted Potatoes

SERVES 4

2 TABLESPOONS FLOUR

4 CENTER-CUT LOIN PORK CHOPS
(¾ INCH THICK, ABOUT 1¾ POUNDS
TOTAL)

1 TABLESPOON OLIVE OIL

2 TEASPOONS UNSALTED BUTTER

1 POUND SMALL UNPEELED RED
POTATOES, HALVED

¼ TEASPOON BLACK PEPPER

2½ T ⅓ CUP PURE MAPLE SYRUP

1½ T 3 TABLESPOONS CIDER VINEGAR

1. Preheat the oven to 425°.

2. Spread the flour in a shallow bowl. Dredge the pork chops lightly in the flour, shaking off the excess.

3. In a large nonstick skillet, warm 2 teaspoons of the oil over medium-high heat. Add the pork chops and cook until browned, about 4 minutes per side.

4. Meanwhile, in a small saucepan, warm the butter until melted. Stir in the remaining 1 teaspoon oil. Place the potatoes in a large baking dish or roasting pan, drizzle the butter-oil mixture over them, and sprinkle with the pepper. Toss the potatoes to coat well.

5. Transfer the browned pork chops to a baking dish large enough to hold them in one layer and cover tightly with foil. Reserve the skillet; do not wash. Place the potatoes in the oven and roast for 10 minutes. Place the pork chops in the oven with the potatoes and bake for 10 to 15 minutes, or until the potatoes are tender and light golden and the chops are cooked through.

6. Meanwhile, add the maple syrup and vinegar to the drippings in the reserved skillet and bring to a boil over medium-high heat, stirring to scrape up any browned bits clinging to the bottom of the pan. Reduce the heat to low, cover, and simmer until the sauce is slightly thickened, about 10 minutes. Remove from the heat and skim off any surface fat.

7. Serve the chops drizzled with the sauce and with the potatoes on the side.

SWEET AND SAVORY SPARERIBS

SERVES 4

1 CUP KETCHUP

¼ CUP TOMATO PASTE

3 TABLESPOONS CIDER VINEGAR

2 TABLESPOONS DIJON MUSTARD

⅓ CUP (PACKED) LIGHT BROWN SUGAR

2 TEASPOONS DRY MUSTARD

3 GARLIC CLOVES, MINCED

12 SPARERIBS, IN TWO RACKS (6 RIBS
    PER RACK, ABOUT 3 POUNDS TOTAL)

1. Preheat the broiler or prepare the grill. If broiling, line a broiler pan with foil.

2. In a small saucepan, combine the ketchup, tomato paste, vinegar, Dijon mustard, brown sugar, dry mustard, and garlic. Bring to a boil over medium heat. Reduce the heat to low, cover, and simmer while you parboil the spareribs.

3. Bring a large skillet of water to a boil. Add the spareribs and return the water to a boil over medium-high heat. Reduce the heat to medium-low, cover, and simmer for 10 minutes. Remove the spareribs with tongs. Place them, bone-side up, on the grill or the prepared broiler pan.

4. Thickly spread about half the barbecue sauce over the ribs. Grill or broil 4 inches from the heat until dark mahogany with some charred patches, about 9 minutes. Turn the ribs over, paint them with the remaining barbecue sauce, and grill or broil about 9 minutes longer.

5. Cut the racks into individual ribs and serve.

KITCHEN NOTE: *Luscious pork ribs are often prepared for grilling by parboiling them. This cooks off some of their fat and also shortens grilling time. In this recipe, the parboiling time dovetails nicely with the simmering of the barbecue sauce.*

BROILED HAM WITH PINEAPPLE AND MUSTARD GLAZE

SERVES 6

◆ EXTRA-QUICK

TWO 8¼-OUNCE CANS JUICE-PACKED
    PINEAPPLE SLICES
3 TABLESPOONS DRY MUSTARD
1 TABLESPOON BROWN SUGAR

¼ TEASPOON GROUND CLOVES
¼ TEASPOON BLACK PEPPER
1½ POUNDS HAM STEAK

1. Preheat the broiler. Line a broiler pan with foil.

2. Drain the pineapple, reserving ¼ cup of the juice. In a small bowl, combine the pineapple juice, mustard, sugar, cloves, and pepper to make the glaze.

3. Place the ham steak on the broiler pan and brush the top with half of the glaze. Broil 4 inches from the heat for 7 minutes, or until golden.

4. Turn the steak over and brush with half of the remaining glaze. Arrange the pineapple rings on top of the steak and brush them with the remaining glaze. Broil 4 inches from the heat for 7 minutes longer, or until the pineapple is light golden around the edges.

SWEET AFTERTHOUGHT: *For a homemade (but extremely simple) fruit sorbet, try this trick: Drain a can of apricot, peach, or pear halves. Dice the fruit and spread it out on a plate lined with wax paper. Place in the freezer until frozen but not rock hard. Place the frozen fruit in a food processor and process to a smooth purée. This should be served as soon after puréeing as possible.*

SALISBURY STEAKS WITH SAVORY SAUCE

SERVES 4

◆ EXTRA-QUICK

¼ POUND MUSHROOMS, COARSELY CHOPPED

2 CELERY RIBS, COARSELY CHOPPED

1 MEDIUM ONION, COARSELY CHOPPED

2 GARLIC CLOVES, MINCED

⅔ CUP FINE UNSEASONED DRY BREAD CRUMBS

1 POUND LEAN GROUND BEEF

½ TEASPOON SALT

¼ TEASPOON BLACK PEPPER

2 TABLESPOONS UNSALTED BUTTER

1 CUP BEEF BROTH

2 TABLESPOONS TOMATO PASTE

¼ CUP CHOPPED CHIVES OR SCALLION GREENS

1. Preheat the broiler. Line a broiler pan with foil.

2. In a large bowl, combine half of the mushrooms, celery, onion, and garlic, and ⅓ cup of the bread crumbs with the ground beef. Add the salt and pepper, and mix well. Form the mixture into patties a scant ½ inch thick. Place the patties on the broiler pan and broil 4 inches from the heat for 5 minutes. Turn over and broil for 7 minutes longer, or until browned on top.

3. Meanwhile, in a medium skillet, warm the butter over medium-high heat until melted.

Add the remaining mushrooms, celery, onion, and garlic to the skillet and sauté until the onion is slightly softened, about 2 minutes.

4. Stir in the broth, tomato paste, and remaining ⅓ cup bread crumbs. Bring to a boil. Reduce the heat to medium-low, cover, and simmer for about 5 minutes (or until the beef patties are finished broiling). Just before serving, stir in the chives.

CHEESE-FILLED PEPPER BURGERS

SERVES 4

◆ EXTRA-QUICK

1 POUND GROUND ROUND

1 MEDIUM ONION, FINELY CHOPPED

2 TABLESPOONS WORCESTERSHIRE OR
STEAK SAUCE

½ TEASPOON SALT

1 TEASPOON COARSELY CRACKED BLACK
PEPPER

¼ POUND SHREDDED MONTEREY JACK
OR PEPPER JACK CHEESE

1. In a medium bowl, combine the beef, onion, Worcestershire sauce, salt, and ¼ teaspoon of the pepper, and mix gently. Divide the hamburger mixture into 4 equal portions.

2. Flatten each portion of hamburger into a patty and press one-fourth of the cheese into the center. Pull the sides of the hamburger patty up and over the cheese to completely enclose it. Gently reform into a flat patty,

making sure the cheese does not poke out. Sprinkle the hamburger patties with the remaining ¾ teaspoon pepper, pressing it gently into the meat.

3. In a large skillet, preferably nonstick, cook the hamburgers over medium-high heat until done: 3 minutes per side for medium-rare, 4 minutes per side for medium, and 5 minutes per side for well-done.

VARIATION: *During grilling season, barbecue the hamburgers instead of pan-frying them. But if possible, use a hinged grilling basket to avoid the risk of breaking the burgers (and letting the cheese run out) when you turn them over. Serve the cheese-filled burgers on toasted buns with beefsteak tomatoes and Bermuda onion rings.*

Classic Beef Fajitas

SERVES 4

◇ LOW-FAT

¼ CUP FRESH LIME JUICE

2 TABLESPOONS TEQUILA OR GIN

½ TEASPOON CHILI POWDER

½ TEASPOON OREGANO

¼ TEASPOON CUMIN

¼ TEASPOON BLACK PEPPER

1 POUND BOTTOM ROUND STEAK, SLICED ACROSS THE GRAIN INTO THICK STRIPS

8 SCALLIONS, TRIMMED BUT WHOLE

1 POUND PLUM TOMATOES, FINELY CHOPPED

1 GREEN BELL PEPPER, FINELY DICED

1 SMALL ONION, MINCED

1 TO 2 JALAPEÑO PEPPERS, MINCED

2 TABLESPOONS CHOPPED CILANTRO

¼ TEASPOON SALT

8 FLOUR TORTILLAS, WRAPPED IN FOIL

2 CUPS SHREDDED ROMAINE LETTUCE

1. In a large shallow dish, combine 2 tablespoons of the lime juice, the tequila, chili powder, oregano, cumin, and black pepper. Add the steak strips and the scallions, and toss them well. Let the steak marinate for 20 minutes at room temperature.

2. Meanwhile, in a bowl, combine the tomatoes, bell pepper, onion, jalapeño pepper(s), cilantro, salt, and remaining 2 tablespoons lime juice. Let the salsa stand for at least 15 minutes to blend the flavors.

3. Preheat the broiler or prepare the grill. If broiling, line a broiler pan with foil.

4. Cook the steak strips in the center of the grill or broiler, with the scallions laid carefully at the side, for 1 minute per side; the steak should be medium-rare and the scallions lightly charred. Warm the tortillas on the grill or in the oven.

5. To serve, cut the steak strips into pieces about 1 inch long. Place equal amounts of steak pieces and their juices on the tortillas. Add some lettuce and a scallion to each tortilla, then spoon some of the salsa over the top. Roll up the tortillas and serve them at once; pass any remaining salsa separately.

Index

Recipes that are marked in the body of the book with the symbol ◆ take 30 minutes or less to prepare. They are grouped in the index under the name Extra-Quick. Recipes that are marked in the body of the book with the symbol ◇ derive 30% or fewer of their calories from fat. They are grouped in the index under the name Low-Fat.

B

Barbecue. *See also Grilled foods*
Barbecued Beef Kebabs, 78
Honey-Apricot Spareribs, 80
Stovetop Barbecued Burgers, 100
Sweet and Savory Spareribs, 121
Beef
Barbecued Beef Kebabs, 78
Beef and Barley Salad with Cherry Tomatoes, 108
Beef and Mushroom Soup, 111
Beef and Mushroom Stir-Fry, 47
Beef and Sausage Balls in Spicy Tomato Sauce, 20
Beef and Tomato Salad, 106
Beef Bourguignon Sauté, 30
Beef Paprikash over Egg Noodles, 13
Beef Stew with Couscous, 15
Beef Tacos with Fresh Salsa, 93
Beef Tossed with Red Cabbage and Apples, 46
Beef with Peppers and Pasta, 9
Beef-and-Onion Shepherd's Pie, 62
Beef-Tomato Curry, 12
Bulgur-Stuffed Red Peppers, 58
Cajun Meat Loaf, 65
Cheese Meat Loaf with Parslied Tomato Sauce, 63
Cheese-Filled Pepper Burgers, 124
Chili with No Beans, 113
Chuckwagon Beef Stew with Dumplings, 114
Classic Beef Fajitas, 125
Dijon Burgers with Grilled Onions, 96
Ginger Orange Beef, 48
Grilled Beef and Avocados in Flour Tortillas, 90
Grilled Beef Gyros with Middle Eastern Salad, 91
Grilled Steaks with Mustard-Yogurt Sauce, 76
Grilled Steaks with Red Wine-Mushroom Sauce, 74
Herb-Marinated Steak, 72
Herbed Steakburgers, 97

Light Beef Stew with Asparagus, 14
Light Fajita Roll-Ups, 92
London Broil Teriyaki, 68
London Broil with Caramelized Onions, 70
London Broil with Chili Seasonings, 67
Marinated Beef Salad, 105
Mexican Burgers with Taco Toppings, 98
Mexican Steak Salad, 104
Mini-Beef Patties with Red Pepper Rice, 99
Oven-Roasted Steak Kebabs with Potatoes, 55
Quick Chunky Chili, 10
Roast Eye Round with Mushroom Sauce, 119
Salisbury Steaks with Savory Sauce, 123
Simple Beef Burgundy, 117
Sirloin and Leek Skewers with Ginger Chutney, 77
Sirloin Steak with Dijon and Herbed Potatoes, 69
Skillet-Roasted Steak with Piquant Sauce, 31
Skirt Steak with Black Bean Chili Sauce, 75
Sloppy Josés, 94
Spicy Oriental Hamburgers with Orange Sauce, 95
Steak with Horseradish-Mushroom Cream, 73
Steak with Lemon-Pepper Crust, 71
Stir-Fried Flank Steak and Vegetables, 49
Stovetop Barbecued Burgers, 100
Tex-Mex Beef Skillet, 11
Thai Grilled Beef Salad, 107
Three-Pepper Smothered Minute Steak, 115
Top Round Sautéed with Broccoli and Cauliflower, 50
Burgers
Cheese-Filled Pepper Burgers, 124
Chili-Topped Pork Burgers, 103
Dijon Burgers with Grilled Onions, 96
Herbed Pork Burgers with Apple-Carrot Relish, 102
Herbed Steakburgers, 97
Lamb Burgers with Basil and Parmesan Sauce, 101
Mexican Burgers with Taco Toppings, 98

Mini-Beef Patties with Red Pepper Rice, 99
Salisbury Steaks with Savory Sauce, 123
Spicy Oriental Hamburgers with Orange Sauce, 95
Stovetop Barbecued Burgers, 100
Veal Patties in Parsley Cream Sauce, 89

C

Chili
Chili with No Beans, 113
Quick Chunky Chili, 10
Chops
Apple-Braised Pork Chops with Red Cabbage, 21
Broiled Pork Chops with Nectarine Chutney, 82
Broiled Veal Chops with Winter Vegetable Sauté, 66
German-Style Pork Chops with Mushrooms, 39
Lamb Chops with Cucumber-Mint Salsa, 86
Maple-Glazed Pork Chops with Roasted Potatoes, 120
Pecan-Mustard Pork Chops, 56
Pork Chops Braised with Onions, 22
Pork Chops Diablo, 41
Pork Chops with Apples and Onions, 40
Pork Chops with Caramelized Apples, 37
Pork Chops with Fresh Cranberry Sauce, 118
Pork Chops with Lemon-Soy Sauce Glaze, 38
Pork Chops with Orange Sauce, 42
Tomato-Grilled Pork Chops, 79
Veal Chops with Sour Cream-Dill Sauce, 29
Veal Chops with Spinach, Tomatoes, and Peas, 28
Cutlets
Gingered Pork Cutlets, 34
Italian Veal and Peppers, 27
Pork Cutlets with Zesty Sauce, 33
Pork Parmesan, 32
Sweet-and-Sour Veal Scaloppini, 25
Veal Cutlets with Lemon and Parsley, 26

E–G

Extra-Quick
Apple-Braised Pork Chops with Red Cabbage, 21
Beef and Mushroom Stir-Fry, 47
Beef Tacos with Fresh Salsa, 93
Beef with Peppers and Pasta, 9
Broiled Ham with Pineapple and Mustard Glaze, 122
Broiled Pork Chops with Nectarine Chutney, 82
Cheese-Filled Pepper Burgers, 124
Dijon Burgers with Grilled Onions, 96
Ginger Orange Beef, 48
Gingered Pork Cutlets, 34
Grilled Beef and Avocados in Flour Tortillas, 90
Hawaiian Pork Skillet, 51
Kielbasa with Apples, Cabbage, and Celery, 24
Light Fajita Roll-Ups, 92
London Broil with Caramelized Onions, 70
London Broil with Chili Seasonings, 67
Milanese Meatball Heros, 88
Orange Pork Stir-Fry, 52
Pork Chops Braised with Onions, 22
Pork Chops Diablo, 41
Pork Chops with Fresh Cranberry Sauce, 118
Pork Chops with Lemon-Soy Sauce Glaze, 38
Pork Parmesan, 32
Pork Strips with Dipping Sauce, 84
Pork Stroganoff, 16
Pork with Apple-Caraway Cream, 43
Quick Chunky Chili, 10
Salisbury Steaks with Savory Sauce, 123
Simple Beef Burgundy, 117
Skillet-Roasted Steak with Piquant Sauce, 31
Skirt Steak with Black Bean Chili Sauce, 75
Spicy Lamb Sauté, 54
Spicy Oriental Hamburgers with Orange Sauce, 95
Steak with Horseradish-Mushroom Cream, 73
Steak with Lemon-Pepper Crust, 71
Stir-Fried Flank Steak and Vegetables, 49
Stir-Fried Lamb with Green Beans, 53
Stovetop Barbecued Burgers, 100
Sweet-and-Sour Veal Scaloppini, 25
Tex-Mex Beef Skillet, 11
Three-Pepper Smothered Minute Steak, 115
Veal Patties in Parsley Cream Sauce, 89
Fajitas
Classic Beef Fajitas, 125
Light Fajita Roll-Ups, 92
German-Style Pork Chops with Mushrooms, 39
Grilled foods
Barbecued Beef Kebabs, 78
Dijon Burgers with Grilled Onions, 96
Grilled Beef and Avocados in Flour Tortillas, 90
Grilled Beef Gyros with Middle Eastern Salad, 91
Grilled Steaks with Mustard-Yogurt Sauce, 76
Grilled Steaks with Red Wine-Mushroom Sauce, 74
Herbed Steakburgers, 97
Honey-Apricot Spareribs, 80
Honey-Glazed Pork Tenderloin, 83
Indonesian-Style Grilled Pork, 81
Lamb Burgers with Basil and Parmesan Sauce, 101
Lamb Chops with Cucumber-Mint Salsa, 86
Lamb Shish Kebab with Yogurt Dipping Sauce, 87
London Broil Teriyaki, 68
Mexican Burgers with Taco Toppings, 98
Sausage and Potato Kebabs with Mustard Glaze, 85
Sirloin and Leek Skewers with Ginger Chutney, 77
Steak with Lemon-Pepper Crust, 71
Sweet and Savory Spareribs, 121
Thai Grilled Beef Salad, 107
Tomato-Grilled Pork Chops, 79
Gyros, Grilled Beef, with Middle Eastern Salad, 91

H–K

Ham
Broiled Ham with Pineapple and Mustard Glaze, 122
Ham and Swiss Cheese Casseroles, 59
Ham Steak with Maple-Bourbon Glaze, 45
Ham-and-Rice-Stuffed Peppers, 61
Indonesian-Style Grilled Pork, 81
Italian Meat Loaf with Tomato Sauce, 64
Italian Sausage and Squash Stew, 17
Kebabs
Barbecued Beef Kebabs, 78
Indonesian-Style Grilled Pork, 81
Lamb Shish Kebab with Yogurt Dipping Sauce, 87
Oven-Roasted Steak Kebabs with Potatoes, 55
Pork Strips with Dipping Sauce, 84
Sausage and Potato Kebabs with Mustard Glaze, 85
Sirloin and Leek Skewers with Ginger Chutney, 77
Kielbasa with Apples, Cabbage, and Celery, 24

L

Lamb
Lamb Burgers with Basil and Parmesan Sauce, 101
Lamb Chops with Cucumber-Mint Salsa, 86
Lamb Shish Kebab with Yogurt Dipping Sauce, 87
Spicy Lamb Sauté, 54
Stir-Fried Lamb with Green Beans, 53
London broil
London Broil Teriyaki, 68
London Broil with Caramelized Onions, 70
London Broil with Chili Seasonings, 67
Low-Fat
Beef Stew with Couscous, 15
Beef Tossed with Red Cabbage and Apples, 46
Beef with Peppers and Pasta, 9
Bulgur-Stuffed Red Peppers, 58
Chuckwagon Beef Stew with Dumplings, 114
Classic Beef Fajitas, 125
Honey-Glazed Pork Tenderloin, 83
Light Beef Stew with Asparagus, 14
Spicy Lamb Sauté, 54

M

Meat loaf
Cajun Meat Loaf, 65
Cheese Meat Loaf with Parslied Tomato Sauce, 63
Italian Meat Loaf with Tomato Sauce, 64
Meatballs
Beef and Sausage Balls in Spicy Tomato Sauce, 20
Hearty Tomato-Meatball Soup, 6
Milanese Meatball Heros, 88
Swedish Meatballs, 19
Milanese Meatball Heros, 88
Minestrone with Chick-Peas, 7

P–R

Paprikash, Beef, over Egg Noodles, 13
Pork
  Apple-Braised Pork Chops with Red
    Cabbage, 21
  Broiled Pork Chops with Nectarine
    Chutney, 82
  Cajun Meat Loaf, 65
  Chili-Topped Pork Burgers, 103
  German-Style Pork Chops with
    Mushrooms, 39
  Gingered Pork Cutlets, 34
  Hawaiian Pork Skillet, 51
  Herbed Pork Burgers with Apple-
    Carrot Relish, 102
  Honey-Glazed Pork Tenderloin, 83
  Italian Meat Loaf with Tomato Sauce,
    64
  Maple-Glazed Pork Chops with
    Roasted Potatoes, 120
  Orange Pork Stir-Fry, 52
  Pecan-Mustard Pork Chops, 56
  Peppered Pork Steaks with Pears, 35
  Pork and Ginger Stir-Fry Salad, 109
  Pork Chops Braised with Onions,
    22
  Pork Chops Diablo, 41
  Pork Chops with Apples and Onions,
    40
  Pork Chops with Caramelized
    Apples, 37
  Pork Chops with Fresh Cranberry
    Sauce, 118
  Pork Chops with Lemon-Soy Sauce
    Glaze, 38
  Pork Chops with Orange Sauce, 42
  Pork Cutlets with Zesty Sauce, 33
  Pork in Wine Sauce, 23
  Pork Parmesan, 32
  Pork Strips with Dipping Sauce, 84
  Pork Stroganoff, 16
  Pork with Apple-Caraway Cream, 43
  Pork-and-Sausage-Stuffed Golden
    Apples, 60
  Red Pepper Pork with Mint, 36
  Roasted Pork Loin Provençale, 57
  Tomato-Grilled Pork Chops, 79

S

Salads, main-course
  Beef and Barley Salad with Cherry
    Tomatoes, 108
  Beef and Tomato Salad, 106
  Marinated Beef Salad, 105
  Mexican Steak Salad, 104
  Pork and Ginger Stir-Fry Salad, 109
  Thai Grilled Beef Salad, 107
  Warm Lentil and Sausage Salad, 110

Salisbury Steaks with Savory Sauce,
  123
Sandwiches. *See also Burgers*
  Grilled Beef and Avocados in Flour
    Tortillas, 90
  Grilled Beef Gyros with Middle
    Eastern Salad, 91
  Milanese Meatball Heros, 88
  Sloppy Josés, 94
Sausages
  Beef and Sausage Balls in Spicy
    Tomato Sauce, 20
  Italian Sausage and Squash Stew, 17
  Kielbasa with Apples, Cabbage, and
    Celery, 24
  Lentil-Sausage Stew, 18
  Pork-and-Sausage-Stuffed Golden
    Apples, 60
  Sausage and Potato Kebabs with
    Mustard Glaze, 85
  Sausages Pizzaiola, 116
  Sautéed Sausage, Mushrooms, and
    Peppers, 44
  Warm Lentil and Sausage Salad,
    110
Scaloppini, Sweet-and-Sour Veal, 25
Shepherd's Pie, Beef-and-Onion, 62
Skirt Steak with Black Bean Chili
  Sauce, 75
Sloppy Josés, 94
Soups
  Beef and Mushroom Soup, 111
  Hearty Tomato-Meatball Soup, 6
  Minestrone with Chick-Peas, 7
Spareribs
  Honey-Apricot Spareribs, 80
  Sweet and Savory Spareribs, 121
Steak
  Grilled Steaks with Mustard-Yogurt
    Sauce, 76
  Grilled Steaks with Red Wine-
    Mushroom Sauce, 74
  Herb-Marinated Steak, 72
  London Broil Teriyaki, 68
  London Broil with Caramelized
    Onions, 70
  London Broil with Chili Seasonings,
    67
  Sirloin Steak with Dijon and Herbed
    Potatoes, 69
  Skillet-Roasted Steak with Piquant
    Sauce, 31
  Skirt Steak with Black Bean Chili
    Sauce, 75
  Steak with Horseradish-Mushroom
    Cream, 73
  Steak with Lemon-Pepper Crust, 71
  Three-Pepper Smothered Minute
    Steak, 115

Stews
  Beef Paprikash over Egg Noodles, 13
  Beef Stew with Couscous, 15
  Beef with Peppers and Pasta, 9
  Beef-Tomato Curry, 12
  Chili with No Beans, 113
  Chuckwagon Beef Stew with
    Dumplings, 114
  Easy Veal Stew, 112
  Italian Sausage and Squash Stew, 17
  Lentil-Sausage Stew, 18
  Light Beef Stew with Asparagus, 14
  Pork Stroganoff, 16
  Quick Chunky Chili, 10
  Tex-Mex Beef Skillet, 11
  Veal Stew with Onions and Mustard,
    8
Stir-fries
  Beef and Mushroom Stir-Fry, 47
  Beef Tossed with Red Cabbage and
    Apples, 46
  Ginger Orange Beef, 48
  Hawaiian Pork Skillet, 51
  Orange Pork Stir-Fry, 52
  Pork and Ginger Stir-Fry Salad, 109
  Spicy Lamb Sauté, 54
  Stir-Fried Flank Steak and Vegetables,
    49
  Stir-Fried Lamb with Green Beans, 53
  Top Round Sautéed with Broccoli
    and Cauliflower, 50
Stroganoff, Pork, 16
Swedish Meatballs, 19

T–V

Tacos, Beef, with Fresh Salsa, 93
Tex-Mex Beef Skillet, 11
Thai Grilled Beef Salad, 107
Three-Pepper Smothered Minute Steak,
  115
Veal
  Broiled Veal Chops with Winter
    Vegetable Sauté, 66
  Easy Veal Stew, 112
  Italian Veal and Peppers, 27
  Milanese Meatball Heros, 88
  Sweet-and-Sour Veal Scaloppini, 25
  Veal Chops with Sour Cream-Dill
    Sauce, 29
  Veal Chops with Spinach, Tomatoes,
    and Peas, 28
  Veal Cutlets with Lemon and Parsley,
    26
  Veal Patties in Parsley Cream Sauce,
    89
  Veal Stew with Onions and Mustard,
    8